NEW TASTES IN GREEN TEA

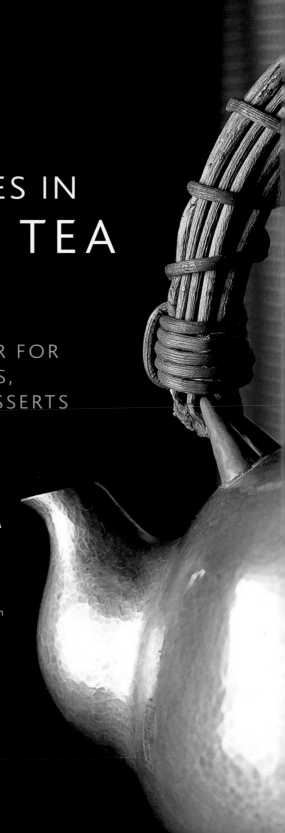

NEW TASTES IN
GREEN TEA

A NOVEL FLAVOR FOR
FAMILIAR DRINKS,
DISHES, AND DESSERTS

MUTSUKO TOKUNAGA

Foreword by Jane Pettigrew

Translated by Yoko Toyozaki and Stuart Atkin

KODANSHA INTERNATIONAL
Tokyo · New York · London

CONTENTS

Photography by Mizuho Kuwata and Kenji Shinohara.

Published by Kodansha International Ltd., 17–14 Otowa 1-chome, Bunkyo-ku, Tokyo 112–8652, and Kodansha America, Inc.

Distributed in the United States by Kodansha America, Inc., and in the United Kingdom and continental Europe by Kodansha Europe Ltd.

ISBN 4–7700–2986–1

First edition, 2004

10 09 08 07 06 05 04   10 9 8 7 6 5 4 3 2 1

FOREWORD

For almost five thousand years, the Chinese have enjoyed the refreshing and rejuvenating qualities of green tea, and today, even in countries that traditionally favor black tea, the interest in green is growing.

Foremost among the factors leading to this new awareness are the remarkable health benefits of green tea, at present being documented in study after study. Spurred on by a fresh wave of interest, supermarkets, tea shops, tea rooms, and hotel lounges around the world now offer an increasing range of fragrant green teas, and manufacturers in tea-producing countries are experimenting with new products, flavorings, and blends to offer the adventurous tea lover an exciting range of new taste experiences.

Ever since tea was first discovered, its cultivation and consumption have been encouraged because of its apparent ability to ward off disease, strengthen powers of concentration, cleanse the body, and aid digestion. Legends of its medicinal properties reached Europe and the New World from China, intriguing the Western consumer, and now, centuries later, modern research has begun to confirm many of those early beliefs.

In the initial phases of tea consumption in Europe and the United States, both black and green teas were regularly drunk. Over time, the British traveled down the tea road while the rest of Europe and the United States gradually turned to coffee. Where tea continued to reign, a preference for black tea won out and led to the almost total demise of green tea in those markets and a decline in knowledge and appreciation of it. But now, Western tea drinkers are once again eager for detailed information on how green teas are grown, manufactured, brewed, and drunk.

My own desire for a deeper understanding of the fascinating qualities of Japanese green tea developed during visits to Japan in the 1990s. On one of my journeys, I met and worked with Mutsuko Tokunaga and found that we shared the pleasure, enjoyment, and satisfaction to be derived from the brewing and drinking of green tea, as well as an appreciation of the tea ceremony and the elegant utensils associated with it. We also discussed the exciting rise of green tea as an everyday ingredient in cooking in Japan, a trend that she thoroughly explores in this book.

With *New Tastes in Green Tea*, Ms. Tokunaga has given us a fascinating and wonderfully instructive book, covering every possible aspect of the story. Since the beginning of the tea renaissance of the early 1980s, many books about tea have been published in various languages and for all types of readers. But the vast majority focus on black tea, perhaps because so many of us were ignorant of the fascinating range of greens. In the past two or three years, writers on tea have begun to include green tea in their musings but, to date, have not discussed the subject—or explored its wealth of possibilities—in as much depth as this book now does. Tea lovers everywhere will find this handsome volume an invaluable addition to their tea library.

Jane Pettigrew

INTRODUCTION
A Green Treasure

Drinking tea—and green tea in particular—punctuates our day with precious and refreshing pauses, whether it is after a satisfying meal or when taking a much-needed break in our busy schedule.

The tea plant that is grown throughout East Asia belongs to the China variety, one of two main types of tea. It is a sturdy, multistemmed bush that grows to a height of eight feet or so (two and a half meters) and is capable of withstanding cold temperatures. In Japan, as in other parts of Asia, tea has been enjoyed for centuries, so much so that it has become deeply interwoven in the lives of the people and has had a strong influence on the development of several important arts and crafts. Wider knowledge of the artistic aspects of green tea has also encouraged awareness of the health benefits of the beverage throughout the world.

A brief glimpse at the history of green tea reveals that in ancient China it was consumed as a herb to treat illness. Later, tea took on religious overtones when Japanese monks visiting China brought the plant back with them and grew it on temple grounds. The Zen priest Eisai (1141–1215) is credited with introducing the custom of tea drinking to Japan in the Kamakura period (1192–1333). In his book *Kissa yojoki* (Health Benefits of Tea) he extols the properties of tea in this famous passage: "Tea is a miraculous medicine for the maintenance of health; it is the elixir that creates the mountain-dwelling immortals."

In the fifteenth century, tea became such a revered beverage that a whole culture developed around it, culminating in the tea ceremony (*cha-no-yu*). The drinking of tea became a highly structured recreation centered on such aesthetic and philosophical concepts as *wabi* (austere beauty) and *sabi* (tranquility). Eventually the tea ceremony became synonymous with cultural refinement, and court nobles and the wealthy would frequently participate in the ritual. It was only much later that the custom of tea drinking spread to the average person and tea became an indispensable daily beverage.

In recent years, green tea has received much coverage in the media as one of the reasons for the longevity of the Japanese, which ranks among the highest in the world. Furthermore, with more scientific evidence on the effectiveness of green tea for certain health problems, its popularity has soared. As a drink that heals the spirit as well as the body, green tea can indeed be called a "green treasure."

Green tea can be a useful part of our daily life—it can be drunk and enjoyed for its soothing effect, and it can be used as a herb in savory dishes and desserts to make full use of its distinctive flavor and aroma. With that in mind, this book presents a variety of innovative recipes for drinks and dishes that incorporate the ingredient.

Green tea plays an integral part in life's three major pleasures—drinking, eating, and cooking. So it is my hope that this book will stimulate you to add your own creative touches to the ideas introduced here, and lead you to find more ways of enjoying tea. Ultimately, I am sure you will share my conviction in the extraordinary allure of green tea in its many forms.

Mutsuko Tokunaga

PART 1

A TEA DRINKER'S GUIDE

SENCHA

FUKAMUSHICHA

KUKICHA

KONACHA

BANCHA

MATCHA

Types of Japanese Green Tea

The term "tea" encompasses an amazing range of different kinds of drinks. First of all, tea can be divided into three broad categories: unfermented, semifermented, and fermented drinks. Green tea is the unfermented type. There are two ways to stop the process of fermentation: one is by steaming tea leaves in a steamer and the other is by roasting (or panning). For the Japanese varieties of tea, the process is almost universally accomplished by steaming.

There are about twenty different types of Japanese tea. The kind most often made in Japan is the steamed type of sencha and fukamushicha, which together account for seventy-five percent of the tea produced in the country. Aromatic teas such as bancha and hojicha are very popular as well. Tea is grown throughout Japan, but the areas that are most well known for their tea are Shizuoka, Kagoshima, and Uji, all of which have types of tea named after them. Many other locales also have their own distinctive local teas with their devoted enthusiasts.

A tea drinker may sometimes want an astringent taste and at other times desires a smooth, aromatic blend. This book sets out to familiarize tea drinkers with the range of possibilities, presenting enough information about the kinds of teas out there and the kind of taste each has, so that the best tea can be selected for the mood or occasion. The world of tea is vast but easily navigated with a little knowledge and a willingness to experiment.

The best way to quickly familiarize yourself with a variety of teas is to find a tea shop that allows patrons to buy small amounts (perhaps as little as an ounce) of many different leaves, as samples. This is very helpful in finding new tastes and selecting favorites. A handful of the most popular types of Japanese tea is presented on the following two pages.

Sencha   *Japan's most popular tea*

The flavors that distinguish sencha are a delicate sweetness and a mild astringency. Sencha refers to the first picking of the tea bush, which takes place from late February in warm climates to the end of May in cooler areas. The tea leaves of later pickings, which have more astringency, constitute the tea known as bancha. The glossy leaves of the tea bush are nearly uniform in size and impart a refreshing fragrance. Sencha is high in vitamin C and is especially popular with women as a teatime drink. A new variety of sencha (*mizudashi-sencha*) specially prepared for steeping in cold water is now available on the market and enjoys brisk sales in summer. Powdered sencha (funmatsucha) is another product on the market, although it is easily made by grinding sencha leaves in a coffee mill or a food processor. It is excellent for adding to drinks and cooked dishes.

Sencha

Fukamushicha   *Ideal for delicate stomachs*

The processing of fukamushicha is the same as for sencha (see pages 54–55), except that for fukamushicha the leaves are steamed two or three times longer. As a result, the leaves become withered, and the color is also darker. However, the taste remains just as "sweet" and moderate, and the fragrance is richer and deeper. Despite the stronger aroma, fukamushicha is gentle on the stomach, and you can drink as many cups as you wish.

Fukamushicha

Kukicha   *A refreshing fragrance to wake up to*

Kukicha consists of stems and stalks normally discarded in the production of sencha, gyokuro, and matcha teas. Kukicha produced from the stalks of gyokuro (see opposite) is known as "karigane" and is highly prized. Kukicha made from either gyokuro or sencha is served in the same way as its base tea. The clean taste and light fragrance are sure to help you wake up feeling refreshed.

Kukicha

Konacha   *Good for cooking with or for sprinkling over dishes*

Konacha (or "tea powder") is the tea served at sushi restaurants, where it is called "*agari.*" It consists of the rejected buds and tea "dust" left over from the processing of sencha and gyokuro. It is reasonably priced and has a strong color, flavor, and aroma, making it an ideal cooking ingredient.

Konacha

Bancha   *A tea that refreshes the palate after meals*

After the first picking for sencha is done from late February to the end of May, new shoots and leaf buds begin to grow, and these are used for bancha. Bancha leaves are picked in June (nibancha), August (sanbancha),

Bancha

and October (yonbancha), with the leaves becoming tougher with each subsequent picking. As well as the leaves, bancha includes the upper stems and some larger leaves discarded during the process of sencha production. Compared to sencha, bancha is more astringent and less fragrant, making it just the right tea to sip after a heavy meal. As it contains more flouride than other teas, it is effective against tooth decay and halitosis. High-grade bancha with less astringency and a pleasant fragrance is known as "senryu." Those tea leaves are also longer and thinner.

Matcha *A tea to go with desserts and Japanese confections*

Matcha

Matcha is the powdered tea used in Japan's formal tea ceremony. In its unpowdered form it is called "tencha." Top-grade matcha is a bright shade of green. As a rule, the lighter green varieties are sweeter and the darker ones more astringent. When the new shoots on the tea bush have two or three leaves, they are shaded from sunlight with straw, reed, or cloth screens for two or three weeks. In the processing of tencha, the leaves are dried after being steamed but are not rolled, unlike most other green teas. During the drying process all the leaf veins and fine stems are removed before the leaves are ground into a fine powder in a mill. As with powdered sencha, matcha completely dissolves in the water when well mixed and thus the leaf is consumed in its entirety, providing more nutrients. Matcha is a popular ingredient in savory dishes as well as desserts.

Gyokuro *A high-grade tea that combats fatigue*

Gyokuro

Rich green gyokuro is a top-grade tea. It owes its sweet, mild flavor to high levels of theanine, an amino acid generated by covering the tea bushes with a reed screen two to three weeks prior to picking. This shields the leaves from direct sunlight and results in leaves that are dark green when dried. It is processed in the same way as tencha (see matcha). Gyokuro contains a lot of caffeine and chlorophyl. Caffeine stimulates the brain and the nervous system, while chlorophyl stimulates tissue growth, resulting in healthy skin.

Hojicha *A mild tea for children and those with a delicate constitution*

Hojicha

Hojicha is produced by roasting bancha or sencha over a high heat, resulting in brownish leaves imbued with a savory fragrance. Since it contains relatively little caffeine and tannin, it is good for children, older people, and those recovering from illness. It can also be served cold in the summer.

Genmaicha *The perfect follow-up to a rich meal*

Genmaicha

Bancha or medium-grade sencha combined with well-roasted and popped brown rice (*genmai*) is known as genmaicha. The rice adds a slightly nutty taste, and its mild flavor makes it the ideal tea to drink after a meal that includes oily or deep-fried foods, such as tempura or Chinese cuisine.

Tea Utensils

These are just a few of the utensils that are often used in Japan to make tea drinking a delicious experience. There are many different kinds of utensils and it is interesting to search for the ones that best reflect your tastes and lifestyle.

Tea scoop   *CHASAJI*

This is used to measure the amount of tea leaves to be poured from the tea canister or tea caddy to the teapot. It is used to scoop the tea, like a spoon. It is most commonly made of bamboo, wood, or metal. In the sencha tea ceremony in particular, a slightly larger scoop known as a *chago* is used. There are some made of bamboo or wood that are carved with scenes from poetry or literature. Shown in the photograph is a *chasaji* made of cherry. A scant scoopful is just one teaspoon, and so it is easy to make a good cup of tea consistently.

Teapot   *KYUSU*

Of all the tea utensils, the pot is the most important, so it is essential to choose one that is the right size (see page 31) for a particular type of tea—whether gyokuro, sencha, bancha, fukamushicha, or another type—and to heat the pot before use. In general, a pot with a rounded bottom is thought to make the most delicious tea because the water and leaves can circulate freely. There are three different positions for the handle; it can be at the back, at the side, or across the top. The back-handled type is the easiest to use.

Tea cups   *YUNOMI*

It is best to select teacups of different sizes for different types of tea. Bancha, which is easy to drink in large quantities, calls for a large teacup, whereas sencha should be drunk from a smaller one, and gyokuro should be savored from a tiny cup. It can be fun to drink Japanese tea from Western cups—from a coffee mug, a demitasse cup, or an ordinary teacup. Just remember that tea is often best served in a cup with a white interior, so that the color of the tea can be seen and enjoyed.

Tea caddy   *CHA-IRE*

The most important utensil for keeping tea leaves fresh is the *cha-ire*, or tea caddy. It is sometimes also referred to in Japanese as the *chashin tsubo*, which means the "jar that holds the heart of the tea." *Cha-ire* used in the home are most commonly round and come in a variety of sizes. They generally have a flat inner lid with a knob beneath the outside decorative lid to keep out moisture, and are usually made of metal. The adjacent photo shows one made of tin. Double-lidded tin caddies have long been thought the most effective means of locking moisture out. Recently tea caddies made of paper have become popular as an environmentally friendly alternative. Whatever your choice, remember that tea leaves are delicate and that they need to be transferred right away to an airtight container and stored in a cool, dry place.

Tea Ceremony Utensils

Matcha is the powdered tea that is ceremonially made and served in cha-no-yu, *or the tea cere-mony. The ceremony has all sorts of rules governing the utensils to be used. But in day-to-day life it is fine to drink matcha from whatever cups you like best. One of the most important elements in tea drinking is simply to have a feeling for the utensils and treat them carefully.*

Tea whisk   CHASEN

The bamboo whisk is used to whip matcha into a frothy con-sistency. Although matcha is a fine powder, it does not dissolve simply by adding hot water but must be whipped into a froth. The bamboo tea whisk has a delicate outer circle and a separate inner circle of thin bamboo fronds that work well to blend the water and powdered tea. Sweeping the whisk all around the tea bowl creates an appetizing froth, which also serves to make the tea milder. If a bamboo whisk is not available, a small egg whisk can be used instead to mix the tea in a nonceramic bowl.

Tea bowl   MATCHA JAWAN

Two types of tea bowl are used for matcha—the flatter, open-shaped bowl for summer and a bowl with a thicker lip and vertical walls used in winter (see adjacent photo). Matcha tea bowls are sometimes described by their shape—cylindrical, flat, or a shoelike shape, to name a few—or by the type of ceramic ware, which includes Raku, Shino, Karatsu, Oribe, and Hagi. Nowadays, some people use matcha tea bowls as small cafe au lait bowls or coffee mugs.

Tea jar   NATSUME

This is a decorative tea jar that holds the matcha during the tea ceremony (distinct from the usual tea caddy). The name comes from the utensil's resemblance to the fruit of the natsume, or Chinese date tree. Natsume can be made from wood, bamboo, or paper and are often lacquered. Arranging the mound of matcha in an attractive way inside the natsume is itself consid-ered an art.

Tea scoop   CHASHAKU

This is a slender tea scoop used to remove tea from the *natsume* tea jar. The *chashaku* is usually made of bamboo, but it can be ivory, wood, or lacquer. It is about 7 inches (18 centimeters) long. Its origins are thought to lie in the similarly shaped medicinal spoons of the Chinese Sung dynasty (1128–1279). With contin-ued use, the bamboo *chashaku* takes on a beautiful patina and greater character.

Making the Perfect Cup of Green Tea

You can only make a perfect cup of green tea by understanding and making full use of the characteristics of each kind of tea leaf. Good tea depends on the quality of the tea leaves and the amount used, the temperature, the amount of water added, and the time the leaves are left to steep before the tea is poured. All these factors are important. The following table is a guide to the best way to serve each type of green tea, although the amount of tea leaves can be adjusted according to your personal preferences and the quality of the tea—the higher the quality, the more leaves you need.

TYPE OF TEA	TEACUPS	AMOUNT OF TEA	WATER TEMPERATURE	AMOUNT OF WATER	STEEPING TIME
Sencha (high grade)	3	2 tsp $^1/_5$ oz (6 g)	176° F (80° C) (drifting steam)	$^2/_3$ cup	2 minutes
Sencha (regular) Fukamushicha Kukicha Konacha	3	2 $^1/_3$ tsp $^1/_4$ oz (7 g)	194° F (90° C) (strong steam)	1 cup	30–60 seconds
Gyokuro	3	3 tsp $^1/_3$ oz (9 g)	140° F (60° C) (slight steam)	$^1/_3$ cup	2–3 minutes
Bancha Hojicha Genmaicha	5	5 tsp $^1/_2$ oz (15 g)	Boiling water	2 $^3/_4$ cups	15–30 seconds
Mizudashi-sencha	5	4 tsp $^2/_5$ oz (12 g)	Cold water	2 cups	Over 10 minutes

Note
1 cup refers to 1 U.S. cup, or 8 fl oz (240 ml).
1 teaspoon refers to a level spoonful.

Sencha and fukamushicha

To brew a cup of sencha use a very small teapot and three small teacups. Warm the teapot and teacups by pouring boiling water into them and discarding after 30 seconds.

For high-grade sencha put 2 teaspoons of tea leaves in the pot and add ⅔ cup hot water (176° F; 80° C). At this temperature, steam in a kettle will drift sideways rather than shoot straight up. Cover the pot and steep 2 minutes before serving. To make regular sencha and fukamushicha, steep the leaves for 30–60 seconds.

The flavor components tend to emerge at 140° F (60° C) and the astringency components at 176°F (80° C). The first pouring will taste lighter than subsequent ones. For this reason, when serving the tea, it is best to pour a little into each cup in turn first, then go back and top off each cup so that the tea in all the cups is of uniform strength and flavor. To make the second serving, use slightly hotter water and steep a little longer.

Note: With high-grade tea, always use hot water below the boiling point (176° F; 80° C) to produce the best results. For medium-grade tea, use hot water at about 194° F (90° C), when steam shoots up strongly. Steep for 1 minute before serving.

Bancha, hojicha, and genmaicha

It is better to use a larger teapot and thicker teacups that will retain heat well.

To make 5 servings of tea, put 5 teaspoons of leaves in a pot, pour in 2¾ cups of boiling water, and steep for 15–30 seconds. With these teas, the secret lies in using boiling water and pouring the tea quickly. The tea tastes best when served immediately after it is poured.

Gyokuro

For gyokuro, use small white porcelain teacups so that you can enjoy the brilliant color of the tea as you drink.

First warm the teapot and teacups by pouring boiling water into them and discarding it after 30 seconds. To make 3 servings, put 3 teaspoons of leaves in the pot and add $\frac{1}{3}$ cup hot water heated to 140° F (60° C), a temperature that feels pleasantly warm when holding a cup between the palms. Steep for 2 or 3 minutes, until the rich flavor is extracted.

Serve by pouring the tea until the very last drop. The second serving should be made with half the steeping time. The attraction of gyokuro lies in its condensed and tasty sweetness, so it is important to extract as much of that flavor as possible.

Mizudashi-sencha

Since this tea is made with cold water, the quality of the water becomes very important as it can have a strong effect on the color, fragrance, and taste of the tea.

To make 5 servings, put 4 teaspoons of mizudashi-sencha in a glass jug. Add 2 cups of cold water and let it steep for at least 10 minutes. Remove the leaves, then place the jug in the refrigerator to chill. This is an ideal drink to serve at dinner time in hot weather. It is not only rich in vitamin C but also gentle on the palate.

Iced sencha

To make 3 glasses of iced sencha, place $2\frac{1}{3}$ teaspoons of sencha leaves in a teapot, add cup of hot water (196° F; 90° C), and let it steep for 2 minutes.

The secret of iced sencha lies in making the tea quite strong. Serve it in a glass filled with ice cubes. Sencha on the rocks is a good way to enjoy the tea's color as well as its fragrance. Iced sencha has little astringency and the color will not change even if it is not drunk immediately.

Although the Japanese have the saying, "Saké is the best medicine," in reality tea may prove to be the more effective cure-all. A cup of green tea with a deep and fresh aroma will relax you emotionally and soothe you mentally. The secret to enjoying green tea lies as much in preparing it with loving care as in using high-grade tea leaves.

It is also important to select the tea according to the time, place, and occasion. Make different teas to suit different moods and purposes. Depending on the occasion, you may want a tea with more bite to it, or one that quenches your thirst, or perhaps a tea to follow a good meal.

Change the leaves often

In order to get the full benefits of tea, it is important to change the tea leaves frequently. Do not keep drinking the tea from the same leaves. If you drink ten cups a day of only the first and second servings of tea, you will be sure to feel the full effects of the tea catechins.

The correct water temperature

Two essential elements to ensure that tea is served at its best are the correct water temperature and the right amount of tea leaves (see page 23). Remember that the catechins and caffeine will dissolve better in water at a higher temperature. There is an old saying that the first serving of tea should be made with water that is not too hot in order to draw out the flavor, and the second serving should be made with hotter water in order to draw out the astringency. Ideally, one should aim for a fine balance between flavor and astringency. Even if the water is not too hot, amino acids, such as theanine (the basis of the flavor) and glutamine, will dissolve in it. Naturally, the correct water temperature varies according to the type of leaves used. The quality of the tea also affects the amount of tea leaves used—the better the quality, the more leaves you need. Ultimately, however, it is a matter of personal preference.

Select the water carefully

The quality and type of water naturally affect the taste of tea. These days some people prefer bottled mineral water to tap water for making tea. Mineral water that has a high mineral content is described as "hard water," compared to "soft water" with fewer minerals. In Japan, spring water is mostly soft and is ideal for green tea. If the water is too hard, the tannin cannot be fully extracted from the tea, and if the water is not hard enough, the aroma cannot be completely released. Thus, it is important to check the minerals listed on the bottle and select a softer water containing less calcium.

Tap water can smell unpleasantly of chlorine, so before using it, boil the water for two or three minutes and let it cool to the right temperature. (You can cool boiling water more quickly by pouring it into another container or teapot.) The smell of chlorine will disappear if the water is left to stand for four or five hours. Let unboiled water stand overnight.

Drink it—don't keep it

When green tea comes into contact with air, it quickly oxidizes, loses its aroma, and darkens in color. Moreover, the vitamin C in the leaves is soon killed off. Tea in an unopened container can be preserved for a longer time; but once the container is opened, the tea should be transferred to a canister with a tight-sealing lid. Store in a refrigerator if possible, but take care that other food smells do not seep into the tea. For these reasons, it is advisable to buy tea in smaller packets, especially if it is high-grade tea.

Choose the right teapot
(SEE PAGE 31)

The flavor of tea also depends on the types of teapot and teacups you select. For high-grade teas, a smaller teapot is best, but for ordinary teas such as bancha an earthenware teapot will retain heat better and produce the best flavor. Don't forget to keep the teapot clean and wash even the difficult-to-reach parts, such as the spout.

Matcha
How to Make and Drink It

Most people automatically associate matcha with the tea ceremony and all the rules and etiquette this entails. But making an invigorating cup of matcha need not involve such formalities and is much easier than you might think. Matcha should be regarded as a healthy type of tea that can be drunk in everyday life.

The items used in the formal tea ceremony include a tea scoop (*chashaku*) for measuring the amount of tea, a bamboo whisk (*chasen*) for mixing the powder smoothly, and the tea bowl (*chawan*). However, it is perfectly satisfactory to substitute these, respectively, with a teaspoon, a small egg whisk, and a small bowl or mug. You will also need a tea strainer to sift the powdered tea.

Begin by sifting the amount of matcha you need. Next, warm the bowl and whisk by setting the whisk in the bowl handle-up and adding water. Wait a minute or so, then discard the water.

Put ⅔ teaspoon (or 1½ heaping tea scoops) of matcha into the tea bowl. Bring some water to a boil and pour ¼ cup into another bowl to cool down to 176° F (80° C), or simply set aside until water cools to desired temperature. When it has cooled to the right temperature, add the water to the matcha. Whisk briskly with one hand while holding the tea bowl in the other. Mix the matcha until a fine foam appears on the surface, which means the tea is smooth and ready for drinking.

THE ETIQUETTE
OF DRINKING MATCHA

There is a saying in Japan that if you drink matcha sitting in a formal posture—that is, with your back straight—he pleasure of the experience will double. Matcha etiquette may seem difficult, but once you know the basic rules, your enjoyment will increase many times over.

Begin by placing the tea bowl on the palm of your left hand. Place the palm of your right hand lightly along the side of the bowl. When serving matcha to a guest, you must turn the bowl clockwise so that the "front" of the bowl (usually showing the main design) faces the guest. Before drinking, the bowl should be rotated in two small clockwise turns, so as not to drink from the front of the bowl. Traditionally, the tea is drunk in exactly three and a half sips.

THE SELECTION OF TEA UTENSILS

The flavor of green tea is subtly influenced by the utensils used. Both teapot and teacups should be attractive in shape and easy to use, and the cup should sit comfortably in the palm.

The Japanese-style teapot, or *kyusu*, originated from a kettle that the Chinese used for warming alcoholic drinks. Japanese teapots are designed so they can be used easily with one hand. Placing a thumb lightly on the lid while pouring will prevent it from falling off and breaking. To make the tea brew more quickly and evenly, you can gently shake the pot by moving it in a circular motion. *Kyusu* are ideal because every last bit of tea can be poured—and not a single drop wasted. The *kyusu* is either lined with a mesh strainer or has a built-in strainer at the base of the spout to prevent the leaves from being poured out with the tea.

Different sizes of *kyusu* are used for different grades of tea. For gyokuro and high-grade sencha, smaller *kyusu* are appropriate. As a general guide, use a *kyusu* with a capacity of $\frac{1}{2}$ cup of hot water for gyokuro, $1\frac{1}{4}$ cups for quality sencha, and 2 to $2\frac{1}{2}$ cups for medium-quality tea.

Slightly larger earthenware *kyusu* are used for genmaicha, hojicha, and bancha, which are made with hotter water. After use, the teapot must be washed carefully, especially the spout.

Choose teacups that have good shape and color and are smooth on the hands and lips. All these elements can affect the taste of the tea. There are two basic types of cups: porcelain and stoneware. Porcelain cups are thinner than stoneware ones and are better for gyokuro and sencha teas; they are served at a temperature lower than boiling, so these thinner cups will not scald your hand. However, as boiling water is used for bancha and hojicha, a thicker stoneware cup is more suitable. Moreover, the tea will retain heat better in that kind of teacup.

Teacups that are white, cream, or light brown on the inside will best display the color of the tea. Serve sencha in a demitasse cup or a regular teacup for a more stylish effect, in a mug if you want to drink a lot, or in a cocktail glass if it is served cold.

Drinking Out
Green Tea Cafes

The tea-drinking experience has expanded tremendously since the olden days in Japan, where roadside tea shops offered the weary traveler a place to rest and relax over a cup of green tea and a bite to eat. Today, tea cafes in metropolitan areas serve a wide range of green tea blends in attractive settings. The high-style chic of Cha Ginza in Tokyo (pages 4–5) as well as the coffeehouse decor of Toraya Café in Tokyo's Roppongi Hills dish up new avenues for the enjoyment of green tea.

Overseas, changes are also brewing. In Manhattan, ITO EN serves an appetizing array of green teas, new blends, and snacks and also sells more than seventy-five types of tea from Japan, China, and elsewhere. Among its mixes are such intriguing hybrids as Earl Grey sencha, vanilla hojicha, and bancha chamomile. Toraya boasts a tea salon in Paris and distributes its traditional tea confectionery to select shops in Europe and the United States. Even in the bastion of black tea, the United Kingdom, black and green tea blends with fruit and spice flavorings are gaining favor.

Addresses for these shops can be found on page 127.

GREEN TEA AND JAPANESE CONFECTIONERIES

In Japan, it is customary to serve confectionery, or *wagashi* (literally, "Japanese cakes"), with green tea. *Wagashi* are very dainty and attractive sweets that are made from riceflour, wheatflour, sweetened adzuki beans, and various seasonal fruits. An important feature of *wagashi* is that they can convey a seasonal touch in the fruit that is used as the motif of their decoration.

There are no hard-and-fast rules about the kind of confectionery served with green tea, but it is worthwhile choosing the cakes according to the type of tea being used, the time, the place, and the occasion.

Sencha goes particularly well with small Japanese dry confectioneries that are not too sweet, or those with a seasonal touch. Bancha, which is more astringent, is better suited to the sweeter Japanese confectioneries. These usually feature red adzuki beans, and popular types are *taiyaki* (a fish-shaped wafer filled with sweet beanpaste) and *daifuku* (riceflour dough around a sweet beanpaste center).

When drinking sencha, it is best to drink the first cup before eating any confectionery so that you can fully appreciate the taste. Conversely, for the tea ceremony, in which matcha is served, it is better to take some confectionery before drinking the tea to counter the bitterness of the matcha. Ordinary confectioneries go well with bancha and should be eaten while drinking the tea.

Western confections also go well with green tea. Recommended combinations include chocolates with matcha, brownies with plain hojicha, jelly beans with sencha, and wafers with bancha.

TEA ON THE GO

With the recent surge of interest in tea among the younger set in Japan, a variety of ready-to-drink green teas—brewed and bottled and fashionably draped with enticing labels—have found their way into markets and vending machines in Japan and Japanese specialty shops overseas.

Traditional Teas — New Tastes

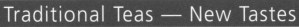

Until very recently, green tea was never drunk with milk or sugar in Japan, or with the addition of any type of liquor. However, the present trend of mixing different styles of cuisine has also influenced green tea. Here are some recipes for green tea drinks that reflect this trend.

Green Tea Latte

INGREDIENTS ———————————————————————— serves 1

1⅓ tsp sencha
1 cup milk
a few dried sencha leaves

1. In a small saucepan, combine the sencha and milk and heat over a low flame, taking care not to let the milk come to a boil. Pour into a cup through a tea strainer.

2. Serve garnished with dried tea leaves.

Matcha Latte

INGREDIENTS ———————————————————————— serves 1

1⅓ tsp matcha + 3 tsp hot water
1 cup milk
1 Tbsp honey

1. Mix the matcha and hot water in a cup, and stir briskly until the paste becomes smooth. (A good rule of thumb is to use twice the amount of water to the amount of matcha.)

2. Heat the milk and honey over a low flame, taking care not to let the milk come to a boil. Combine with the matcha paste and stir until well blended.

Sencha with Vodka and Lime

INGREDIENTS ──────────────────────────────── serves 1

2 tsp mizudashi-sencha (brewed with cold water)
¾ cup water
2 Tbsp gin or vodka, or to taste
1 slice lime

1. Make the sencha by adding the cold water and letting it sit several minutes until the flavor is released.
2. Mix with either gin or vodka in any ratio you like, and serve with a slice of lime.

Gyokuro Tea with *Shochu*

INGREDIENTS ──────────────────────────────── serves 1

1 tsp gyokuro
3 Tbsp *shochu* or vodka
⅓ cup hot water

1. Put the gyokuro tea into a glass and add the liquor.
2. Add hot water and stir to mix.

The brilliant green color of the drink may tempt you to a few more glasses. The softened tea leaves may also be eaten afterward.

Note
1 cup refers to 1 U.S. cup, or 8 fl oz (240 ml).
1 teaspoon or tablespoon refers to a level spoonful.

Salty Dog Matcha

INGREDIENTS ———————————— serves 1

juice of half a grapefruit   3–4 ice cubes
2 Tbsp vodka, or to taste   ½ tsp matcha
⅓ tsp salt

1. Squeeze the grapefruit to extract the juice. Moisten the rim of a glass with the rind and dip rim in salt. Fill the glass with ice cubes.
2. Place the grapefruit juice, vodka, and matcha in a cocktail shaker, and shake until well mixed.
3. Pour over the ice cubes and serve immediately.

Matcha and Banana Shake

INGREDIENTS ———————————— serves 1

1 tsp matcha   1 banana
1 cup milk   honey to taste

1. Mix all the ingredients in a blender to make this breakfast drink.
2. Add ice to taste, if desired.

Matcha Yogurt Drink

INGREDIENTS ———————————— serves 1

1 tsp matcha + 2 tsp hot water
3–4 ice cubes   ½ cup plain yogurt
½ cup cold milk   sugar to taste

1. In a large glass or cup, mix the matcha and 2 teaspoons of hot water, and stir briskly until the paste becomes smooth. Add the ice cubes.
2. Combine the yogurt, milk, and sugar, and stir until well blended.
3. Pour into the glass and stir well.

Note
Instead of the yogurt and milk, you can use a carbonated drink such as ginger ale to make a refreshing matcha-flavored soft drink. Adjust the amount of matcha according to taste.

Matcha Float

INGREDIENTS ——————————————————————————— serves 1

2 tsp matcha + ½ cup of hot water
5–6 ice cubes
½ cup cold milk
1 scoop vanilla ice cream
syrup or low-calorie sweetener, to taste

1. In a tall glass, mix the matcha and hot water, and stir briskly until the paste becomes smooth.
2. Add the ice cubes and pour the milk slowly over them.
3. Top with ice cream. Add some syrup or sweetener if you wish. Serve with a long spoon.

Note
To counter the sweetness of the ice cream, use more matcha.

Green Tea Viennese

INGREDIENTS ——————————————————————————— serves 1

1 tsp matcha (or 1 tsp sencha, powdered in a mill)
1 cup hot water
sugar or honey to taste
2 Tbsp fresh cream, whipped

1. Heat a cup of water to 176° F (80° C).
2. Add hot tap water to cup to warm. Discard water.
3. Mix the matcha and 2 tsp hot water, and stir briskly with a tea whisk or small egg whisk until the paste becomes smooth.
4. Pour in the rest of hot water, stir, and add sugar.
5. Serve topped with whipped cream.

Matcha Smoothie

INGREDIENTS ———————————— serves 1

½ cup plain yogurt

2 Tbsp honey, sugar, or low-calorie sweetener

½ cup frozen apple or pineapple

1 tsp matcha   ⅓ cup crushed ice

1. In a blender, combine the yogurt, honey,
   and frozen fruit and blend until smooth.

2. Sprinkle on the matcha, add the crushed
   ice, and mix well.

Note
Cut the fruit into bite-size pieces before freezing.
Allow 10 minutes for the fruit to soften before
putting the pieces in the blender to avoid damaging the blades.

Iced Matcha au Lait

INGREDIENTS ———————————— serves 1

1 tsp matcha

1 Tbsp sugar

¼ cup hot water

¾ cup cold milk

3–4 ice cubes

6-inch (15-cm) stalk of lemon grass

1. Mix the matcha with the sugar, add the
   hot water, and stir until the paste becomes smooth.

2. Add the cold milk and stir. Add the ice
   cubes.

3. Serve with the lemon grass for added
   flavor.

Matcha Yogurt Sour

INGREDIENTS ———————————— serves 1

1 tsp matcha + 2 tsp hot water

3 Tbsp milk

1 Tbsp condensed milk

½ cup yogurt

½ peach, fresh or canned

3–4 ice cubes

6-inch (15-cm) stalk of lemon grass

1. Mix the matcha and hot water, and stir
   briskly until the paste becomes smooth.

2. In a blender, combine the milk, condensed milk, yogurt, and peach. Blend
   until smooth.

3. Fill a tall glass with ice cubes and pour
   the mixture over them. Top with a few
   drops of matcha paste and serve with
   the lemon grass for added flavor.

Matcha Coconut Drink

INGREDIENTS ———————————— serves 1

1 tsp matcha + 2 tsp hot water

⅔ cup milk

⅓ cup coconut milk

1 Tbsp sugar

a little aloe or any cut fruit

1. Mix the matcha and hot water, and stir
   briskly until the paste becomes smooth.

2. Add the milk, coconut milk, and sugar,
   adjusting the proportions according to
   taste.

3. Serve garnished with diced aloe or your
   favorite fruit.

G reen tea, drunk throughout the day, is an indispensable part of the daily life of the Japanese. Today, however, people are adding new tastes to their favorite drink by combining green tea with black teas, herbs, and spices. This new trend of blending and flavoring is expanding the potential of tea.

Mixing tea with various ingredients is a common practice in many parts of the world: China has "flower teas," such as jasmine tea or chrysanthemum tea; India and the Middle East have *chai*, which is black tea spiced with ginger, cinnamon, cumin, cardamom, and cloves; and Morocco has its famed mint tea. Japan's flavored teas include ginger tea (*shogacha*), pickled plum tea (*umeboshicha*), which protects against colds, and tea mixed with bonito flakes (*bushicha*), which is a great stamina-booster. All these teas have been drunk since ancient times and aid blood circulation and general metabolism.

Heat-resistant glass teapots are recommended for making herbal teas. For teas that require boiling, use a small saucepan and a tea strainer.

Standard quantities for a herbal tea are 2 cups of water, 1 teaspoon of matcha or powdered sencha, and 2 teaspoons of ground herbs or ⅔ teaspoon of dried herbs (for fresh herbs, double the quantity). Naturally, the amounts may be changed to suit your taste.

First warm the teapot and add the herbs and tea. Pour in the hot water, replace the lid, and wait 10 minutes or so until the medicinal components are

Herb Tea Blends

Whispering Breeze
(For 2 cups of hot water)

Mix 1 teaspoon of matcha or powdered sencha with fresh herbs such as 5 pine-apple sage leaves and 2 laurel leaves.

Song of the Earth
(For 2 cups of hot water)

Mix 1 teaspoon of matcha or powdered sencha with 1 thyme sprig, 5 lavender flowers, and 5 sage leaves.

Sunlight
(For 2 cups of hot water)

Mix 1 teaspoon of matcha or powdered sencha with 5 mint leaves and 5 lemon balm leaves. One alternative is to use chamomile or red rose petals.

Forget-me-not Tea
(For 2 cups of hot water)

Mix 4 teaspoons of hojicha and 2 rosemary sprigs. The aroma of roasted hojicha perfectly balances the strong fragrance of rosemary. This tea refreshes the mind.

Green and Black Tea Blends

Blending different types of tea provides all the excitement of taking part in a treasure hunt. Although their tastes differ, green tea, Chinese oolong tea, and black tea are close relatives and mix well. Interesting and distinctive flavors can be achieved by blending aromatic black teas and tasty green teas in a variety of ways.

Basic Blend

1 tsp (heaping) green tea (ordinary sencha or hojicha)
⅓ tsp black tea of your choice
2 cups hot water

You might want to add a ½ teaspoon of your favorite dried herbs (double the amount if fresh herbs are used). The amount of tea and herbs can be adjusted to taste. On the facing page are some other suggestions.

Variations

Freshen your skin

Add ⅙ tsp lemon grass, some blue mallow flowers, and red rose petals to the basic blend.

For a good night's sleep

Add ⅓ tsp lime and ⅓ tsp chamomile to the basic blend and drink as a nightcap.

Tomorrow is another day

This blend will help you forget your troubles and give you a lift. Add 2 sprigs of mint and a dash of your favorite alcoholic drink, such as apricot liqueur or *umeshu* plum wine, to the basic blend.

A revitalizing touch of mint

Add 3 sprigs of fresh mint to the basic blend.

A refreshing after-meal drink

Add 3 sprigs of fresh mint and 2 slices of lemon to the basic blend.

Getting a jump on the day

Add 1 tsp fresh thyme and 2 slices of orange to the basic blend.

A sweet aroma for relaxation

Add 3 strawberries to the basic blend.

FRUIT AND FLOWER TEAS

Several traditional teas are drunk in Japan during festivals and to mark the changing seasons.

PLUM BLOSSOM TEA (February):
Pickled plum tea (*umeboshicha*) mixed with plum petals.

DOLL'S FESTIVAL TEA (March):
A combination of matcha and dried peach.

CHERRY TEA (April–May):
Sencha flavored with salted cherry blossoms.

umeboshi

AROMA OF EARLY SUMMER (May–June):
Sencha or matcha flavored with orange and mint.

***YUZU* TEA** (October–March):
Yuzu (Japanese citron) with *kobucha* (tea made from powdered dried kelp).

JASMINE SENCHA (any season):
Sencha mixed with jasmine flowers.

ORCHID TEA (any season):
Sencha with salted orchid petals.

LYCHEE TEA (any season):
Sencha flavored with fresh or frozen lychees.

yuzu

PART 2

ALL ABOUT
GREEN TEA

The Cultivation of Tea Bushes

Tea plantations provide some of the most memorable vistas in east Asia. Few visitors will ever forget the sight of row upon row of rounded, neatly trimmed tea bushes stretching into the distance like an endless expanse of surging waves.

The tea plant—*Camellia sinensis*—belongs to the genus *Thea* and is closely related to the *Camellia sasanqua,* well known for its attractive white or red flowers. If left to nature, tea plants will also produce flowers, although somewhat smaller than the famous flowering camellias.

South China's Yunnan Province is home to some enormous tea trees that date back over a thousand years. It is thought that they were once cultivated and then left to grow wild. As the habit of tea-drinking became more popular, tea plants were improved and different species suited to each region were developed.

There are two main varieties of tea bushes—China and Assam. The China variety is a multistemmed bush that grows to a height of eight feet (two and a half meters) and has small roundish leaves. It is a sturdy plant that can withstand the cold. These plants are mainly cultivated in China and Japan to produce oolong tea or green tea.

The Assam variety has larger leaves and is more sensitive to the cold. It is more like a tree, with a single stem that can grow to a height of between twenty and sixty feet (five and eighteen meters), but the domesticated variety is constantly pruned to keep the plants low so the leaves are easier to pick. This variety is cultivated in tropical areas such as India and Sri Lanka, and the leaves are processed to produce black tea.

Tea plants can bear having their leaves picked as many as three or four times a year. After the first crop has matured, cuttings are taken, consisting of mature sprigs with two nodes. These are planted in cutting beds where humidity and moisture in the soil are controlled. After a year, when the cuttings have grown to about six inches (fifteen centimeters) in height, they are transplanted to open fields. Nowadays, paper pots are used so the cuttings can be transferred from nursery to field without damaging the roots. A tea bush reaches maturity between the seventh and tenth year, which is the time when the plant produces the best-quality leaves.

In the past, tea leaves were always hand-picked. Pickers would pinch off clusters of two young leaves and a needle-shaped shoot, referred to as "a leaf set with bud," and toss them into a basket strapped to their back. In Japan, tea-picking was usually carried out in rhythm with special songs, such as this one:

> Summer approaches indeed.
> Eighty-eight nights have passed
> Since the start of spring.
> Over there are the tea-pickers,
> Wearing their red sashes and sedge hats.

Today, however, it is machines that do the picking. Although machines can work more quickly and efficiently than hand-pickers, they are unable to distinguish between old leaves and new leaves. Picking starts as early as late February in warm areas, such as Okinawa, and continues through mid-May as the warm weather advances north. In the tea-growing region of Shizuoka the first crop, or "shincha" (new tea), is ready for picking in May, on the eighty-eighth day after the onset of spring in early February. This crop provides the highest grade of green tea because the leaves are young and tender.

After every picking the tea plant sends out new leaves, and between two and four crops are harvested in a year. As fall approaches, the leaves become progressively tougher, resulting in poorer-quality tea. Thus, the lower grades of the second, third, and fourth crops generally supply the tea known as "bancha." Once the last crop is picked, the tea bushes are pruned and readied for the following year.

Most agricultural crops are grown on low-lying plains, where abundant sunshine gives high yields, but tea bushes grow better in hillier areas, where the air is cooler and there is a greater diurnal range in temperature. Another factor essential for good tea is the soil, the best being that which is well-drained and slightly acidic. Thus, humid areas situated on hillsides near a river or stream are ideal for tea plantations.

Japan's most famous tea-growing districts are all located near rivers and experience misty or hazy conditions in the mornings and evenings. These regions are mainly in Shizuoka Prefecture—in the center of the main island of Honshu—and in Saga Prefecture, on the large southern island of Kyushu.

Famous tea brands grown in these districts include Kawane-cha (upper reaches of the Ohi River Shizuoka Prefecture), Tenryu-cha (upper reaches of the Tenryu River Shizuoka Prefecture), Hon'yama-cha (upper reaches of the Abe River, Shizuoka Prefecture), Uji-cha (along the Uji River, Kyoto), Yame-cha (Fukuoka Prefecture), and Ureshino-cha (Saga Prefecture).

Because of the mists, these regions have fewer hours of sunshine, which reduces the astringency in the leaves and at the same time increases the flavor-enhancing amino acids (theanine and glutamic acid). In tea plantations

situated on low-lying plains with a lot of sunshine, the bushes are covered with reed screens or straw mats to shield them from direct sunlight. The highest-grade teas, such as gyokuro and tencha, are particularly sensitive to strong light. When sunlight is blocked out, most of the nutrients absorbed through the roots remain in the leaves, thus increasing the theanine and glutamic acid content.

In his book *Life with Tea* (published by Shisosha), Yozo Tanimoto, an Osaka tea merchant, says: "The production of fine tea requires a good balance between the weather, the soil, and the wisdom and experience of our predecessors—in other words, the perfect harmony between Heaven, Earth, and Man."

The Processing of Sencha

Sencha processing consists of six stages, beginning with the steaming of the tea leaves and ending with the final (third) drying. To protect the leaves from damage, as soon as they are plucked they are transported to a large storage bin, which is equipped with a fan, humidifier, and other machinery. The leaves are kept in constant cool air with a high humidity for three to eight hours, until they are ready for steam-heating. All the types of green tea follow the same basic procedure in their processing, except for tencha—used to make matcha—where the leaves are steamed and dried but not rolled.

1. Steaming

This takes place inside a machine equipped with a net drum and a stirring shaft enclosed in a long steaming drum. The leaves are steamed at a temperature between 176° and 194° F (80° and 90° C) to destroy the oxidizing action of the enzymes and so preserve the green color, the aroma, and the natural astringency of the leaves. Once this process is finished, the water content of the leaves has been reduced to 75 percent.

2. First drying

The steamed leaves are dried in a machine with an air-heating furnace, then

pressed and shot with hot air until the moisture content is further reduced to about 50 percent.

3. First rolling
The tea leaves are stuffed inside a machine with a revolving jacket. Without the action of heat, the leaves are twisted so as to break the cells in them. This renders the leaves soft and pliant and helps maintain a uniform moisture content.

4. Second drying
A machine with a rotary drum is equipped with a furnace. The leaves are placed inside the drum for pressing and drying. This reduces the moisture content to about 30 percent.

5. Second rolling
This pressing and heating process dries the leaves until the moisture content is down to approximately 13 percent. It is at this stage that the leaves assume their characteristic needle shape and the fragrance is produced.

6. Third, final drying
This is done in a machine consisting of a hot-air furnace and drying chamber. The water content is uniformly reduced to 6 percent while maintaining the quality and fragrance of the leaves.

All these processes are usually carried out by the tea farmer before the tea is weighed and packed for transportation to retailers.

The Main Types of Tea

The taste, appearance, and nutritional components of the three types of tea are the result of different processing methods. While green tea is unfermented, black tea is fermented and oolong tea is semifermented.

Green tea is unfermented, meaning that the fresh tea leaves are not oxidized during processing and the green color is retained. Immediately after being picked, the leaves are steamed to deactivate the oxidizing enzyme as quickly as possible and "kill" the leaves. Once oxidation and browning have been halted, the leaves are rolled into thin needle shapes and then dried. This method effectively seals in all the nutritional components of the leaf. The process does not destroy the vitamin C in the leaves, which is one of the main reasons green tea is considered better for the health than black tea or oolong tea.

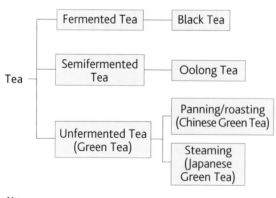

Note
A small portion of Japanese tea products use the panning method.

"Black tea" refers to fermented tea. This involves processing that is the complete opposite of that for green tea. The fresh leaves are first "withered"—dried in direct sunlight or by unheated air being pumped through a layer of leaves. They are then rolled to break up the cells on the leaf's surface to promote oxidation, which results in the aroma and the dark color. Finally, the leaves are heated in iron pans and dried several times to prevent further oxidation. The rolling process—essential in the production of all three types of tea—ensures more efficient infusion when hot water is poured over the leaves.

Oolong tea is semifermented, which means that the leaves are "withered" in the sun and also indoors to reduce the moisture content. When oxidation has reached about 30 percent, the leaves are heated in an iron pan to prevent further oxidation. In the semifermentation process the leaves are prevented from turning black as they do in the case of black tea.

Both black tea and oolong tea contain fewer vitamins than green tea, although to different extents. This is due to the oxidation of the leaves in the withering process: less oxidation takes place in semifermented tea than in fermented black tea. In black tea, vitamin C—considered the most beneficial component—disappears completely.

A Short History of Tea

The first tea plants were grown in Yunnan Province in southern China. From there they spread to other parts of Asia that possessed the right soil and weather conditions. The custom of drinking tea is said to have originated in China with the mythical emperor Shen Nong. Regarded as the father of Chinese medicine, he introduced the tea plant to people around the year 2700 B.C. The classic on Chinese tea, *Cha jing* (The Book of Tea),

Lu Yu deeply involved in his research.

written by the scholar Lu Yu in A.D. 760, recounts Shen Nong's efforts to discover the medicinal efficacy of over three hundred varieties of grasses, roots, and tree bark. It is said that he would try all of them on himself first, and whenever he ingested something poisonous, he would purge himself by eating tea leaves.

It seems certain that tea leaves were initially eaten as a medicine long before tea became a popular drink. There are some hill tribes in southern China, Thailand, and northern Myanmar that still eat pickled tea leaves, and until recently they were unaware that a drink could be brewed from the same leaves.

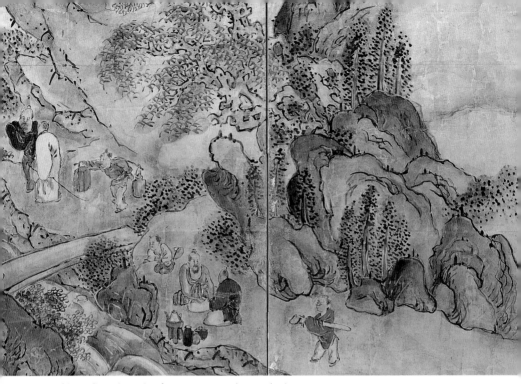

Chinese literati pausing for tea at an outdoor gathering.

According to *Kouga*, an early dictionary written during the Later Han dynasty (A.D. 25–220), people in Sichuan Province, western China, compressed steamed tea leaves into hard bricks to preserve the quality of the tea over a long period. When making a drink, they would season the brew with ginger or onion. However, this early concoction would not qualify as a beverage in the conventional sense because its intended use was medicinal.

In the Three Kingdoms period (221–65), the popularity of tea increased more rapidly. One reason for this was Buddhism, which was beginning to gain a wider following. It prohibited the drinking of alcohol and so stimulated a demand for tea.

During the Sui dynasty (581–618), the custom of drinking tea, previously limited to the aristocracy and Buddhist monks, began to filter through to other classes. In the mid-eighth century, tea shops sprung up, and gradually tea became an indispensable beverage for ordinary city-dwellers.

It was around this time that Lu Yu, who came from the tea-producing center of Hubei Province, wrote his treatise on tea. The range of Yu's work was impressive. It covered the origins, the methods of cultivation, the utensils, the best ways to prepare and drink tea, and anecdotes relating to tea and tea-growing centers. His compendium of information on tea ran to three volumes, opening with this auspicious sentence: "There are good luck trees in the south that are beneficial to a person's health." The book met with high acclaim when it appeared, and is still revered today as the bible of tea.

Tea arrived in Japan from China, brought by Japanese Buddhist monks who accompanied the special delegates dispatched to China in the early Heian period (794–1185). Among the monks who traveled to China were Saicho (767–822), Kukai (774–835), and Eichu (743–816). The first record of the custom of tea-drinking in Japan appeared in *Nihon koki* (Notes on Japan), compiled in the Heian period. Eichu, a priest at the temple of Bonshakuji in Omi, Aichi Prefecture, returned from China in 815. The *Nihon koki* records that when Emperor Saga (reign, 809–23) visited Omi, Eichu invited him to his temple and served him sencha, suggesting that drinking tea, a popular pastime in Tang times, had become fashionable in Japan's intellectual circles as well. *Ryoun-shu*, an anthology of Chinese poetry written in Japanese in 814, also mentions tea-tasting.

At that time, tea probably came in the form of hard bricks, as described by Lu Yu. Compressed into a brick shape, tea was not only easy to transport but it also held up better during the long voyage from China. This was most likely the type of tea brought to Japan, even though leaf tea was also used

in China at that time. The brick was first warmed over a flame and then a portion was broken off by hand or shaved off with a knife. The shavings were ground in a mortar into a coarse powder, which was added to a pan or kettle of hot water and brewed, then served in a tea bowl.

Emperor Saga tried to encourage the spread of tea by ordering provinces in the Kinki region around Kyoto to cultivate the plant. He established tea gardens in one district of Kyoto, and started growing and processing it for the use of physicians attached to the court. This imperial tea, however, found use mostly in rituals performed by the aristocracy; the beverage had yet to become an item for consumption by the common people.

Ordinary Japanese only began to drink tea much later, after Eisai (1141–1215), the founder of the Rinzai sect of Zen Buddhism, brought back a new type of seedling from Sung-dynasty China. With it he introduced a new way of drinking tea, which was known as the "matcha style." Eisai encouraged the cultivation of tea trees, and his *Kissa yojoki* (Health Benefits of Tea) tied tea-drinking to longevity and launched tea in Japan on a large scale.

Eisai's other claims about the benefits associated with tea-drinking certainly contributed to tea's rise in popularity. He noted its ability to dispel intoxication, quench thirst, and facilitate digestion, as well as its diuretic effects and its general efficacy against ailments.

Tea processing at that time closely paralleled the procedure used today for producing tencha (from which matcha is made), where the leaves are steamed and dried but not rolled. As for the style of drinking, it resembled that followed in the present-day tea ceremony. First, the tea leaves were pounded and ground into powder in a mortar. This powder was put into a teacup and hot water poured over it. The liquid was then mixed with a whisk until frothy, and drunk. The simplified preparation recommended by Eisai also led to a spread in consumption.

Another memorable personality connected with tea was Myoe (1173–1232), a Kegon-sect priest at the temple of Kozanji in Kyoto. Using tea seeds he received from Eisai, he devoted himself to spreading both his faith and tea-drinking across the nation. Gradually, from being a special concoction favored for certain rituals and medical treatments, tea evolved into a more common beverage.

Tea plantations continued to be established in the Muromachi period (1392–1568), and tea-ceremony gatherings became more frequent, particularly among the warrior class that had risen to power. It was in this period that Japan's traditional tea ceremony (cha-no-yu) began. Representing a fusion of tea with man's spiritual side, the tea ceremony is a highly formalized event that combines artistic creativity with sensitivity to nature and social interaction. In planning a tea ceremony, every single detail—from the utensils used and the decoration of the tearoom to the ingredients in the meal served before the tea—is carefully orchestrated.

However, the tea ceremony held among the warrior class often took the form of a game in which heavy bets were placed as members tried to guess the provenance of the tea. These gatherings took the form of elaborate banquets, where saké was served. Such entertainments reached a zenith of popularity during the rule of Ashikaga Yoshimasa, the eighth shogun, between 1449 and 1473.

A Zen priest by the name of Shuko Murata (1422–1502) found such frivolous gatherings too removed from the tea-drinking held in Zen temples, where the beverage was enjoyed simply for its taste. He designed the small tea room and advocated a style of tea ceremony based on the ideals of Eisai and incorporating the spirit of Zen Buddhism.

However, it was Sen no Rikyu (1521–91) who devised the style of tea ceremony that has survived to the present. Rikyu was official tea master to the de facto ruler Nobunaga Oda (1534–82) and his successor, Hideyoshi Toyotomi (1537–98). Although Rikyu had presided over more lavish ceremonies, he later came to focus on tea's simplicity. In one of his poems, he reminds his students that "the tea ceremony is nothing more than boiling water, making tea, and drinking it." His rustic and simple style of tea had a strong influence on various arts and crafts, such as pottery, garden design, and Japanese cuisine.

Later, in the Edo period (1603–1867), tea-ceremony gatherings where matcha was served grew more formal and ritualized. At the same time, the custom of drinking sencha—made by pouring hot water onto tea leaves—spread among commoners. Green tea became an everyday item, with people drinking it at any hour of the day as well as at social gatherings.

By the mid-nineteenth century, the methods of processing sencha had improved so much that all the types, colors, and varieties of tea that we know today were being produced.

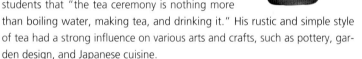

THIS PAGE: Traditional tea bowls by Shiro Tsujimura.

LEFT: Detail from print by Harunobu, eighteenth century.

PART 3

COOKING
WITH
GREEN TEA

Green Tea in Cooking

The Japanese have a long tradition of drinking green tea, either after meals or with midmorning or afternoon snacks. In recent years, however, green tea has not only been enjoyed as a relaxing beverage but has also become a popular seasoning for cooking, just like any other herb.

When used as an ingredient, green tea needs a little preparation due to the catechins in the leaves, which can be bitter-tasting and rough on the palate. However, with a little technique and practice, various kinds of savory dishes and desserts that make full use of the flavor, color, and "bite" of tea can be prepared. If you are concerned about using too much sugar in desserts, you may substitute low-calorie sweeteners.

Green tea can be used in several kinds of cuisine: Japanese, Western, and Chinese. Sencha contains considerable amounts of vitamins A, C, and E, as well as dietary fibers. The vitamin C in green tea is heat-resistant and—aided by the presence of catechins—is better retained during cooking than the vitamin C in vegetables and fruits. You may also find it more convenient to use sencha in powdered form as a cooking ingredient. It is easily ground to powder in a coffee mill or a blender. Matcha comes as a powder to start with, so it is ready to be added as an ingredient just as it is. With its mellow taste and pleasing aroma, matcha is extremely versatile and is thus featured in many dishes presented here.

The following is a list of the different types of tea that can be used to flavor savory dishes as well as desserts.

Tea leaves from the first serving

The remains of high-grade tea leaves after one serving have a gentle taste and retain their bright color. Thus, they can be used in the same way as any parboiled green vegetables. Add them to rice pilafs and salads, or mix them into the batter of deep-fried dishes.

Tea broth

Tea broth refers to the liquid that remains after the tea leaves have been discarded. It should therefore be about the same strength as normal tea that is drunk. When cooled, tea broth is excellent for washing fish in as it removes both the odor and the sliminess. Boiling whole small fish in tea broth makes the flesh more tender.

Powdered sencha

Powdered sencha is very easy to make in a coffee mill or a blender just before use. It dissolves easily in hot water, and can either be drunk as it is or added in liquid form as a seasoning in savory dishes or desserts. Sencha has more astringency than matcha.

Matcha

This is the high-grade powdered green tea used in Japan's formal tea ceremony. It is produced by removing the leaf veins and fine stems to ensure that no tough fibers are left. The leaves are then ground into a fine powder. This is also why matcha costs more than other teas. Matcha is highly nutritious because the whole leaf is consumed when drunk.

To make matcha, add twice the amount of hot water to tea, and stir briskly until it turns into a smooth paste, with no lumps. A bamboo whisk or a small egg whisk is ideal for doing this. The paste can be prepared for a drink or it can be added to a variety of savory dishes, soups, cakes, sauces, and syrups.

Matcha for cooking

A product that is specially designed for cooking purposes is available in a few stores in the United States under the name MT. This is matcha sweetened with oligo-saccharide, which makes it easier to dissolve in foods and renders it less bitter at the same time. MT can either be drunk or mixed with herbs to make herbal teas, where its vivid color is a distinct advantage.

Tencha

Tencha consists of top-grade tea leaves that are ground into matcha. Because the leaves are from the young shoots picked first, they are tender and mild tasting and are excellent to eat. Their fresh color and the lack of an aftertaste allows them to be cooked and served in the same way as any green vegetable.

A tea leaf consists of 77 percent water and 23 percent solid matter. Of the latter, about one-third is made up of water-soluble components—including amino acids, polyphenol (includes catechins), polysaccharides, and vitamin C—and two-thirds consists of insoluble components—including crude fibers, cellulose, vitamin E, and carotene. Each component has its own good qualities, and some, particularly the catechins that generate the astringency of tea, have many other benefits. Some nutrients that are not extracted when tea is steeped in hot water can be used to the full when tea is used as a cooking ingredient.

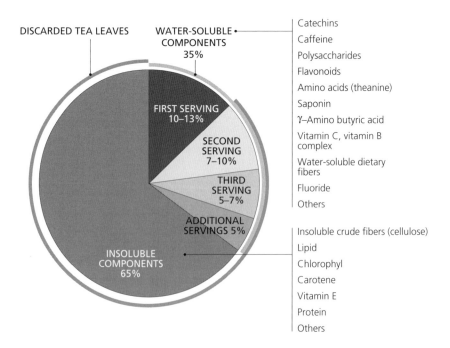

DISCARDED TEA LEAVES

WATER-SOLUBLE COMPONENTS
35%

FIRST SERVING
10–13%

SECOND SERVING
7–10%

THIRD SERVING
5–7%

ADDITIONAL SERVINGS 5%

INSOLUBLE COMPONENTS
65%

Catechins
Caffeine
Polysaccharides
Flavonoids
Amino acids (theanine)
Saponin
Y–Amino butyric acid
Vitamin C, vitamin B complex
Water-soluble dietary fibers
Fluoride
Others

Insoluble crude fibers (cellulose)
Lipid
Chlorophyl
Carotene
Vitamin E
Protein
Others

CATECHINS

Catechins are the agents responsible for the astringency in tea, more commonly called "tannin." Catechins are related to flavonoids, have antibacterial and anti-oxidative functions, and are effective in reducing oxidation, inhibiting the spread of cancer and tumors, and lowering cholesterol levels in the blood. They also play a part in stabilizing blood pressure and blood sugar, resist viruses, and have a deodorization function.

CAFFEINE

The caffeine content of tea leaves is three times higher in the top shoot than in the lower stalk. It is estimated that 1 pound (450 grams) of tea leaves—sufficient to make 200 cups of tea—contain approximately ½ ounce (16 grams) of caffeine. However, the caffeine in green tea is supposedly milder than that in coffee. Caffeine counteracts fatigue and drowsiness, stimulates heart function, and also acts as a diuretic.

POLYSACCHARIDES

Effective in lowering blood sugar.

FLUORIDE

Protects the enamel of teeth and prevents cavities.

VITAMIN B COMPLEX

Effective in regulating the metabolism of saccharine.

VITAMIN C

Its effects include lessening stress and building up resistance to mild infections such as colds.

VITAMIN E

Its effects include an anti-oxidization action and slowing of the aging process.

γ-AMINO BUTYRIC ACID (GAVA)

Protects against hypertension.

FLAVONOIDS

Their effects include strengthening the walls of blood vessels and preventing halitosis.

THEANINE

One of several amino acids, which are responsible for the distinctive aroma and flavor of Japanese tea.

RECIPES

- 1 cup refers to 1 American cup, which is 8 oz (or 240 ml).
- 1 teaspoon or 1 tablespoon refers to a level spoonful.

Five Matcha Spreads ——————————————— serves 2–4

Matcha can be useful to prepare and stock a variety of sweet or savory spreads, such as the ones below. Simple to make, they are delicious on hot toast, focaccia, pancakes, or any kind of bread. Note that the amount of matcha in the recipes can be adjusted according to taste.

Matcha Butter

INGREDIENTS

4 oz (120 g) butter or margarine
½ tsp matcha
4 plain muffins, store-bought

1. Take the butter out of the refrigerator 20 minutes before use to let it soften. Mash with a fork until smooth.

2. Add the matcha powder (approximately 1.5% of the weight of the butter), and mix into the butter until well blended.

3. Slice muffins horizontally and toast in an oven toaster (or oven preset at 340° F; 170° C) until slightly brown. Spread the matcha butter over the hot muffins and serve.

Matcha Condensed Milk Spread

INGREDIENTS

½ tsp matcha + 1 tsp hot water
½ cup condensed milk

1. Mix the matcha and hot water and stir briskly until the paste becomes smooth.

2. Add to the condensed milk and stir until blended. Use as a sweet spread on toast, French toast, pancakes, or rye bread.

Matcha Honey

INGREDIENTS

½ tsp matcha + 1 tsp hot water
½ cup honey, any kind

1. Mix the matcha and hot water and stir briskly until the paste becomes smooth.

2. Add to the honey and stir until blended to make this tea-flavored spread.

Matcha Cream Cheese

INGREDIENTS

4 oz (120 g) cream cheese
½ tsp matcha + 1 tsp hot water

1. Take the cream cheese out of the refrigerator 20 minutes before use to let it soften. Mash with a fork until smooth.

2. Mix the matcha and hot water and stir briskly until the paste becomes smooth.

3. Add to the cream cheese and mix until the color turns a refreshing green.

Matcha Whipped Cream

INGREDIENTS

1 tsp matcha + 2 tsp hot water
½ fresh cream

1. Mix the matcha and hot water and stir briskly until the paste becomes smooth.

2. Lightly whip the cream. Add the matcha to the cream halfway through the whipping. Continue whipping until fluffy. Use as a spread on toast or French toast, or serve with apple pie. It can also be used for decorating cakes, or to top cold drinks such as iced coffee and mint tea.

Matcha Potage

INGREDIENTS ———————— serves 2–4

1 cube chicken consommé
1 cup water
1 cup soy milk
2 servings of instant potage soup
½ tsp matcha + 1 tsp hot water

1. Place the consommé cube in a small pan, add 1 cup of water, and heat over a low flame until the cube dissolves. Add the soy milk and heat until just before boiling point.

2. Add the instant potage soup and stir slowly until it dissolves.

3. Mix the matcha and hot water and stir briskly until the paste becomes smooth.

4. Spoon matcha paste onto the soup to make an attractive pattern. Serve hot.

Green Tea Omelet (or Sandwich)

INGREDIENTS ———————————————— serves 4

1 medium potato

3 oz (90 g) sausages

vegetable oil for frying

1 oz (30 g) processed cheese, any kind

4 eggs

2 Tbsp milk

1 tsp tencha or sencha

salt and pepper to taste

2 Tbsp butter

4–8 cherry tomatoes

a few leaves of fresh mint, fresh basil, or any
    other herb

MATCHA SAUCE

    1 tsp matcha + 1 Tbsp warm milk

    4 Tbsp mayonnaise

    2 Tbsp plain yogurt (low sugar)

1. Cut the potato into ½-inch (1-cm) cubes and cook 2 minutes in a microwave oven until soft. Set aside.

2. Cut the sausages into ½-inch (1-cm) segments. Pour a little oil in a fry pan and fry sausages over low to medium heat until cooked. Set aside.

3. Cut the cheese into ½-inch (1-cm) cubes.

4. Beat the eggs. Add the milk and tea, season with salt and pepper, and mix well. Combine the potato, sausages, and cheese with the eggs.

5. Heat the butter in a fry pan. Over medium-high heat cook the eggs quickly, stirring all the time. Shape into an omelet and put on a serving dish.

6. Make the matcha sauce by mixing matcha and warm milk and stirring until the paste becomes smooth.

7. Combine the mayonnaise and the yogurt, and add the matcha paste.

8. Pour the sauce over the omelet and serve with cherry tomatoes and any fresh herbs.

Note

Omelet with green tea sauce is also excellent served on a slice of any kind of bread, together with a few lettuce leaves.

Matcha Rolls

INGREDIENTS ———————— makes 8 rolls

⅔ cup milk

1 oz (30 g) butter

1 oz (30 g) sugar

1/4 oz (7 g) dry yeast

7 oz (200 g) bread flour (high-gluten)

1 tsp salt

1⅓ tsp matcha, or 3 tsp MT

2 Tbsp sesame seeds

1 Tbsp tea leaves for topping

8 small sausages, optional

1. Warm the milk, add the butter, and stir until it melts. Add the sugar and let the mixture cool down to body temperature.

2. Add the dry yeast and stir. Leave for about 5 minutes until it begins to bubble.

3. Combine the flour, salt, and matcha, and sift into a mixing bowl. Slowly pour in the milk and yeast mixture and knead into a dough.

4. Cover the dough with a kitchen cloth and leave to rise in a warm place for about 40 minutes.

5. When the dough triples in size, divide it into 8 portions and leave to rise for another 30 minutes again.

6. Preheat the oven to 360° F (180° C).

7. Shape the dough into round balls. Place on a baking sheet and leave for 20 minutes to rise for the third time. (Roll out the dough into stick shapes, if you prefer.)

8. Using your fingertips, wet the top of the dough with a little water, and sprinkle with sesame seeds and tea leaves, or any dried herbs. Bake for 12–15 minutes. (If you are making bread sticks, one alternative is to place a sausage inside the stick of dough and bake.)

Light Quiche

INGREDIENTS ———————— for an 8-inch (20-cm) quiche

SHORT CRUST PIECRUST

    9 oz (250 g) all-purpose flour

    $\frac{2}{3}$ tsp salt

    4 oz (115 g) butter

    1 egg yolk

    3 Tbsp cold water

FILLING

    10 oz (300 g) mushrooms, any kind

    $\frac{1}{2}$ oz. (15 g) butter

    salt and pepper to taste

    2 oz (60 g) bacon

    3 eggs

    1 cup milk

    $\frac{1}{2}$ cup fresh cream

    $\frac{1}{2}$ tsp powdered tea, any kind

1. Preheat the oven to 340° F (170° C).

2. Combine the flour and salt and add the butter, cut up into small pieces. With your fingertips blend the butter into the flour until the flour becomes loose and flaky. Add the egg yolk and cold water and knead into a dough. Leave for 30 minutes or so.

3. Roll out the dough into a thin sheet ($\frac{1}{8}$ inch/3 mm). Line a quiche mold and trim off the excess. Bake the piecrust in the oven for 10 minutes.

4. Make the filling by finely slicing the mushrooms. In a fry pan, sauté the mushrooms in butter over low heat until soft, season with salt and pepper, and place in the piecrust.

5. Cut the bacon into thin strips and place over the mushrooms.

6. Beat the eggs, and add the milk, cream, salt, and pepper. Pour mixture into the piecrust and bake at 360° F (180° C) for 30 minutes until brown on top. Serve with a sprinkling of powdered tea for extra flavor.

Matcha Noodle Salad

INGREDIENTS ——————— serves 4

NOODLES

2 tsp matcha + 4 tsp hot water

7 oz (200 g) bread flour

2 eggs

1 Tbsp olive oil

$\frac{1}{2}$ tsp + 2 tsp salt

flour for dusting

2–4 cherry tomatoes

a few lettuce or chicory leaves,
    or shredded celery

SALAD DRESSING

1 tsp salt and pepper to taste

3 Tbsp wine vinegar

5 Tbsp salad oil

1. Mix the matcha and hot water and stir briskly until the paste becomes smooth.

2. Combine the matcha paste, flour, eggs, olive oil, and $\frac{1}{2}$ teaspoon salt. Mix and knead into a dough. Leave for 40 minutes.

3. Roll out the dough as thinly as you can into one large sheet. Sprinkle flour over the top and fold the dough over itself several times, in accordion fashion. Cut into thin strips ($\frac{1}{8}$ inch/3 mm) and quickly loosen the noodles so they don't stick together.

4. Make the dressing by combining the salad ingredients and stirring until mixed.

5. Bring a large pan of water to a boil. Add 2 teaspoons salt and boil the noodles until al dente (2–3 minutes).

6. Drain in a colander and rinse quickly in cold water. Drain again.

7. Place the noodles in a large dish, add the dressing, and mix. Serve with cherry tomatoes and a few lettuce or chicory leaves.

Note

Noodles taste best when eaten immediately after they are boiled.

Green Tea Gnocchi

INGREDIENTS ———————————————— serves 4

18 oz (500 g) potatoes
salt and pepper to taste
1 oz (30 g) butter
1 egg, beaten
2½ oz (75 g) cake flour (low-gluten)
2 tsp powdered sencha or matcha
flour for dusting
1 Tbsp olive oil + olive oil for frying
1 Tbsp salt
1 clove garlic
3–4 tsp grated parmesan cheese
white pepper to taste
mint

1. Peel the potatoes and cut into quarters. In a pan of boiling water with some salt added, boil the potatoes until they are cooked. Drain in a colander.

2. While the potatoes are still hot, season with salt and pepper, add the butter, and mix. Let them cool a little, add the beaten egg, and mix with a wooden spoon.

3. Combine the flour and powdered tea and sift over the potatoes. Mix and knead into a dough, taking care not to knead too much, and shape into a ball.

4. Dust with flour and divide the dough into 3 or 4 portions. Roll each portion into a long strip ½ inch (1 cm) wide, and cut into 1-inch (3-cm) segments.

5. Lightly press each segment with the back of a fork to make grooves.

6. In a large pan of boiling water, add 1 tablespoon of olive oil and the salt. Boil the gnocchi over low heat until they float to the surface. Drain in a colander.

7. Finely slice the garlic. Heat olive oil in a large fry pan and fry the garlic until the aroma is released. Add the gnocchi and mix. Serve immediately, garnished with parmesan cheese, pepper, and mint.

Green Tea Pilaf Rolls

3 Tbsp sencha

3 Tbsp + 3 tsp vegetable oil for frying

3 oz (90 g) ground pork

1 oz (30 g) carrots, finely chopped

2 oz (60 g) bamboo shoots or celery,
  finely chopped

1 tsp + ½ tsp salt

2–4 small bowls of cooked rice

1 tsp soy sauce

3 eggs

2 tsp cornstarch + 1 Tbsp cold water

lettuce leaves and radishes

1. Place the tea leaves in a small pot and add enough hot water to cover. Leave for a few minutes until the leaves become soft. Drain the leaves and set aside.

2. Heat 3 tablespoons of oil in a wok and stir-fry the pork, carrots, and bamboo shoots over high heat. Add 1 teaspoon of salt and the drained tea leaves, and mix. Add the cooked rice and stir-fry for a few minutes. Season with soy sauce, remove from heat, and set aside.

3. Beat the eggs and add ½ teaspoon salt.

4. In a separate bowl, dissolve the cornstarch in cold water and add to the eggs.

5. Heat 3 teaspoons of oil in a fry pan. Pour a little egg into the pan and quickly make a very thin egg sheet 6–8 inches (15–20 cm) in diameter. Continue making sheets until all the egg is used up.

6. Place a little rice pilaf on each sheet and carefully make a neat roll. Make as many rolls as there are sheets.

7. Cut into bite-size pieces, and serve on a dish with lettuce and radishes.

Matcha Cream Cheese Chicory Boats

INGREDIENTS ———————————————————— serves 4

7 oz (200 g) cream cheese

$1\frac{1}{3}$ tsp matcha + 3 tsp hot water

8–10 chicory leaves

1 medium tomato, peeled and diced

watercress or parsley for garnish

1. Remove the cream cheese from the refrigerator 20 minutes or so before use to allow it to soften.

2. Mix the matcha and hot water and stir briskly until the paste becomes smooth. Add to the cream cheese and blend thoroughly with a fork.

3. Place the cream cheese in a pastry tube and squeeze a little on each chicory leaf.

4. Place on a dish, top with diced tomato, and serve with fresh watercress or parsley.

Sardine and Green Tea Canapés

INGREDIENTS ———————————————————— serves 4

4 slices sandwich bread, any kind

butter to taste

1 can of sardines, in oil

1 tsp sencha or matcha

2 Tbsp mayonnaise

1. Cut each slice of bread into four long strips. Lightly toast and butter each strip, and top with sardines.

2. Sprinkle the sardines with sencha leaves and decorate with mayonnaise.

Note

The green tea reduces any fish odor.

Matcha Tofu

1 Tbsp (8 g) agar-agar
1⅔ cups milk
½ tsp salt
2 tsp matcha + 4 tsp hot water
2½ cups water
4 slices lemon or lime
radish, sliced

DRESSING
  ½ cup milk
  2 tsp sugar
  ½ tsp salt
  2 tsp cornstarch + 1 Tbsp cold water
  1 Tbsp apple vinegar

1. Soak the agar-agar in cold water for about 20 minutes to soften. Wring out.

2. In a small pan, heat the mixture until the agar-agar dissolves. Add the milk and salt, and mix. Remove from heat and set aside to cool to 120° F (50° C).

3. Mix the matcha and hot water in another cup and stir briskly until the paste becomes smooth. Add to the cooled mixture and mix well. Put into a square pan around 5 x 5 inches (12 x 12 cm) and place in the refrigerator to set.

4. When set, cut into long thin strips and place in a serving dish.

5. Heat the dressing ingredients (milk, sugar, salt) in a small pan. Add the corn-starch dissolved in cold water. Remove from heat and set aside to cool. Add the apple vinegar.

6. Serve with sliced lime or lemon and radish.

Note
You may use any other dressing you like.

Tofu Salad with Matcha Dressing

INGREDIENTS ——————————————— serves 4

1 cake soft tofu (silk)
3–4 red lettuce leaves
$\frac{1}{2}$ small red onion
1-inch (3-cm) piece of carrot

MATCHA DRESSING

    salt and pepper to taste
    3 Tbsp vinegar
    3 Tbsp salad oil
    2 Tbsp yogurt
    1 Tbsp mayonnaise
    1 tsp matcha or powdered sencha

1. Wrap the tofu in kitchen cloth and let it drain for 30 minutes by putting it on a cutting board placed at a slant. Cut into bite-size pieces and refrigerate.

2. Tear the lettuce leaves into small pieces. Slice the onion thinly and place in cold water for 10 minutes to crisp. Cut the carrot into thin slivers.

3. Make the dressing by combining the salt, pepper, vinegar, and oil. Stir and mix thoroughly.

4. Add the yogurt, mayonnaise, and matcha to the dressing and mix.

5. Place the chilled tofu on a dish together with the lettuce, onion, and carrot. Pour the dressing on and toss just before eating.

Green Tea Croquettes

INGREDIENTS ———————— makes 12 croquettes

4–5 medium potatoes

$\frac{1}{2}$ medium onion

2 Tbsp butter

7 oz (200 g) hashed beef

salt and pepper to taste

pinch of nutmeg

3 Tbsp green peas

1 Tbsp powdered sencha or matcha

$\frac{3}{4}$ cup flour

1 egg, beaten

$1\frac{1}{2}$ cups bread crumbs

vegetable oil for deep-frying

3 oz (85 g) cabbage, finely shredded

1 cherry for garnish

1. Peel and quarter the potatoes and boil in a large pan of water with some salt added. When cooked, drain and mash the potatoes while still hot. Set aside.

2. Finely slice the onion. Heat the butter in a fry pan and sauté the onion over low heat until tender. Add the hashed beef and stir vigorously until the meat breaks up into strands. Season with salt, pepper, and nutmeg, and cook until all the liquid has evaporated. Add the peas and mix.

3. Add the beef to the mashed potatoes. Add the powdered sencha and mix. Then place in a shallow tray to let it cool.

4. Divide the mixture into 12 portions and shape into croquettes.

5. Place the flour, egg, and bread crumbs in 3 separate bowls. Roll each croquette in the flour, dip in egg, and coat with bread crumbs.

6. Heat the oil to 360° F (180° C) and deep-fry the croquettes until they become golden brown.

7. Place the shredded cabbage in the center of a large dish, garnish with a cherry, put the croquettes around it, and serve immediately.

Chicken with Vegetables and Matcha Sauce

INGREDIENTS ———————————————— serves 4

14 oz (400 g) chicken thighs, deboned

salt, pepper, and fresh thyme to taste

1 Tbsp salad oil

4 Tbsp white wine

1 sachet bouquet garni

2 oz (60 g) broccoli, cut into bite-size pieces

vegetable oil for frying

2 oz (60 g) zucchini, sliced into rounds

2 oz (60 g) red pimentos, cut into strips

2 oz (60 g) yellow pimentos, cut into strips

fresh tea leaves or herbs as garnish

MATCHA SAUCE

    3 rounded Tbsp mayonnaise

    3 Tbsp milk

    1 tsp matcha

    salt and pepper to taste

1. Prick the chicken all over with a fork. Season with salt, pepper, and thyme, and leave for 20 minutes.

2. In a fry pan, add the oil and fry the chicken skin-side down over medium heat, taking care not to let it burn. When the skin turns golden brown, turn the chicken over and fry the other side.

3. When brown, add the wine and bouquet garni, cover with a lid, and cook for a few minutes until the chicken is cooked through.

4. Place the broccoli in a pan of boiling water with some salt added and boil for 4–5 minutes.

5. In a fry pan, add some oil and sauté the zucchini and red and yellow pimentos.

6. Make the matcha sauce by combining the mayonnaise and the milk. Add the matcha and season with salt and pepper.

7. Serve the chicken with the vegetables and matcha sauce. Garnish with a fresh sprig of tea leaves or any herb.

Matcha Seafood and Mushroom Gratin

INGREDIENTS ——————————— serves 4

1 Tbsp butter

3 Tbsp chopped onion

7 oz (200 g) shrimps

4 oz (120 g) scallops or oysters

4 oz (120 g) mushrooms

salt and pepper to taste

2 Tbsp white wine

1 tsp grated parmesan cheese

1 tsp bread crumbs

$\frac{2}{3}$ tsp sencha

MATCHA SAUCE

    2 Tbsp butter

    2 Tbsp flour

    2 cups milk

    salt and pepper to taste

    $1\frac{1}{2}$ tsp matcha + 3 tsp hot water

1. In a large fry pan, heat the butter and sauté the onion over medium heat for 2 minutes. Add the shrimps and scallops and sauté for 1–2 minutes, until the shrimps turn red. Add the mushrooms and sauté for 1–2 minutes.

2. Season with salt and pepper and add the wine. Cover with a lid and cook for 2 more minutes. Remove from heat and set aside.

3. Make the matcha sauce in the same way as a béchamel sauce by melting the butter in a small pan. Over very low heat, add the flour and stir until the mixture turns into a smooth ball. Take care not to let it burn.

4. Add the milk in little dribbles at first, stirring vigorously all the time so that no lumps form. Continue adding the milk and stirring until all the milk is used up and the sauce becomes thick and smooth. Season with salt and pepper.

5. Mix the matcha and hot water and stir briskly until the paste becomes smooth. Mix into the sauce and flavor with the juice from the cooked seafood.

6. Heat the oven to 400° F (200° C).

7. Place the seafood in a buttered casserole dish and cover with matcha sauce. Top with parmesan cheese and bread crumbs, and bake for 10 minutes until the top browns.

8. Serve with a sprinkling of sencha leaves.

Salmon and Sencha Pie

INGREDIENTS ——————————————— serves 4

2 salmon steaks

salt to taste

2 Tbsp white wine

2 frozen pie sheets

2 tsp sencha

1 egg, white and yolk separated

1. Cut the salmon steaks in two to make four portions, season with salt, and leave for 10 minutes.

2. Put the salmon in a nonstick fry pan. Over high heat add the wine, cover immediately with a lid, and cook for 2–3 minutes. Remove the skin if you wish.

3. Preheat the oven to 400° F (200° C).

4. Roll out the pie sheets and cut into 4 strips, each measuring 5 x 10 inch (12 x 25 cm). Place a piece of salmon to one side of each sheet and sprinkle some sencha on top. Brush on a little egg white along the edges of the sheet and fold the other side of the pie sheet over the fish. Seal the edges by pressing firmly so they stick together. You can shape the pie into a fish and decorate the surface with a fish-scale pattern.

5. Add a little water to the egg yolk and brush over the pastry. Bake for 15–20 minutes, until brown.

Ochazuke with Salmon Flakes

INGREDIENTS ——————————————————— serves 1

$\frac{1}{2}$ salmon steak

salt to taste

1$\frac{1}{2}$ cups hot water

1$\frac{1}{2}$ tsp sencha, bancha, or hojicha

1 bowl warm cooked rice

2–3 trefoil (*mitsuba*), cut into 1$\frac{1}{2}$-inch (4-cm) lengths

1 Tbsp croutons or any crunchy cereal

Japanese horseradish (*wasabi*), optional

1. Season the salmon with salt and leave for 10 minutes. Broil or grill 5–6 minutes, until slightly brown. Remove the skin and bones, if any, and break up the flesh into flakes.

2. Make the tea broth by adding hot water to the tea leaves.

3. Place the rice in a large bowl and sprinkle salmon flakes over the rice. Add the trefoil, croutons, and, if you wish, a dab of horseradish.

4. Pour as much hot tea as you want onto the rice and eat immediately.

Note

Ochazuke tastes even better when accompanied by good-quality Japanese salted pickled vegetables or any Western-style pickles. Cold *ochazuke* is recommended for summer. For this, use iced sencha, mizudashi-sencha, or any type of green tea that has been cooled down.

ABOUT *OCHAZUKE* (TEA OVER COOKED RICE)

Sukiyaki, tempura, sushi, and yakitori are typical Japanese dishes that are known throughout the world. Some food experts may want to add *ochazuke* to the list.

Ochazuke is a dish in which hot tea is poured over cooked white rice topped with a few simple ingredients. It is a deceptively simple yet extremely tasty dish beloved by all Japanese. *Ochazuke* can be enjoyed as a light meal or snack at any time of day, and it is extremely easy to prepare. All you need to do is put some simple ingredients on a bowl of hot white rice and pour a cup of tea over it.

Of course, the flavor of the dish will improve if you are particular about the rice,

the type of tea, and the topping. Favorite Japanese toppings are pickled plums (*umeboshi*), dried sea laver (*nori*), grilled salmon, soy-simmered fish and seaweed, tempura, broiled eel, and so on. Alternatives from Western cuisine are grilled chicken, grilled salmon, pickled cucumber, smoked salmon, and oysters marinated in oil.

Various seasonings can be added for flavor, such as sesame seeds, Japanese horseradish (*wasabi*), or freshly grated ginger. *Ochazuke* is normally served in a bowl large enough to hold the rice and a generous amount of tea. Individual salad bowls, large breakfast cups, or cereal bowls are good substitutes.

Matcha Ice Cream

INGREDIENTS ———————————— serves 6

2 cups milk

4 egg yolks

⅔ cup sugar

1 Tbsp cornstarch

⅓ tsp salt

4 Tbsp matcha + ⅔ cup hot water

1 cup fresh cream

1 medium orange, cut into sections

fresh cherries

1. Heat the milk in a small pan to about 140° F (60° C). Remove from heat and set aside.

2. Place the egg yolks in a pan and beat lightly. Add the sugar, cornstarch, and salt, and mix thoroughly with a whisk. Gradually pour in the heated milk and stir, making sure that no lumps form. Strain the mixture and pour it back into the pan.

3. Place the pan over a low flame and cook until the milk thickens, stirring all the time with a wooden ladle. Remove from heat and set aside.

4. Mix the matcha and hot water and stir briskly until the paste becomes smooth.

5. In another bowl, whip the cream until semi-stiff, fold into the milk, and add the matcha paste.

6. Pour into a metal or plastic container, and place in the freezer to set. After two hours or so, take it out and mix thoroughly with a spoon or whisk, then resume freezing. Repeat this process 3 or 4 times to ensure the ice cream is smooth.

7. Serve with orange sections and cherries.

Matcha Syrup for Vanilla Ice Cream

INGREDIENTS ———————————— serves 6

4 oz (120 g) sugar

⅓ cup water

2 tsp cornstarch + 4 tsp cold water

1 Tbsp matcha + 2 Tbsp hot water

½ tsp Curaçao or any other liqueur

1. Place the sugar and water in a pan and heat until the sugar dissolves.

2. Mix the cornstarch and cold water and stir until the cornstarch dissolves. Add to the pan and heat until syrup thickens. Set aside to cool.

3. Mix the matcha and hot water and stir briskly until the paste becomes smooth. Pour into the syrup and splash in a little Curaçao for extra flavoring. Mix well.

4. Use as a topping for vanilla ice cream.

Matcha Chiffon Cake

INGREDIENTS ——————————— serves 6–8

4 oz (115 g) cake flour (low-gluten)
2 tsp baking powder
⅓ tsp salt
2 tsp matcha
¼ cup + ¼ cup + 1 Tbsp sugar
3 egg yolks
4 Tbsp vegetable oil
⅓ cup water
4 egg whites,
1 cup fresh cream, whipped

1. Sift together the flour, baking powder, salt, and matcha.

2. Add ¼ cup sugar to the egg yolks and beat until the mixture turns whitish. Add the oil and water and mix.

3. Gradually add the sifted flour to the mixture and knead lightly into a dough. Do not allow it to become too sticky.

4. In a separate bowl, thoroughly beat the egg whites and add ¼ cup sugar. Continue beating until the mixture stiffens like a meringue. Fold into the dough, stirring carefully so that the bubbles do not disappear.

5. Heat the oven to 340°–360° F (170°–180° C)

6. Pour the dough into a spring-form cake pan, and lightly tap the bottom a few times to remove trapped air. Bake for 35 or 40 minutes and remove from the oven.

7. Place the pan upside down and let it cool.

8. Add 1 tablespoon of sugar to the fresh cream and whip. When the cake cools, remove from the pan and decorate with fresh whipped cream.

Matcha Scones

INGREDIENTS ———————————— makes 8 scones

9 oz (250 g) cake flour   1 Tbsp baking powder
⅓ tsp salt   1 tsp matcha
1 Tbsp granulated sugar   2½ oz (70 g) butter
⅗ cup milk
1 egg, separated into yolk and white
strawberry jam and fresh whipped cream to taste

1. Sift together the flour, baking powder, salt, matcha, and sugar.

2. Cut the butter into small pieces. With your fingertips, mix the butter into the flour until it becomes dry and flaky.

3. Combine the milk and egg yolk, and pour the mixture into the flour a little at a time. Mix and knead into a moist dough, but not so moist that it becomes sticky.

4. Preheat the oven to 360° F (180° C)

5. Place the dough on a floured board and knead slightly until smooth. Roll out to a thickness of 1 inch (2 cm) and cut out shapes with a cookie cutter or the rim of a glass.

6. Brush the tops with a little egg white, place on a baking sheet, and bake for 12–15 minutes, until slightly brown.

7. Cut each scone in half and eat with jam and fresh cream.

Steamed Matcha Cupcakes

INGREDIENTS ———————————— makes 8 cupcakes

7 oz (200 g) hotcake mix   ⅔ cup milk
4 Tbsp sugar   1 Tbsp raisins
1½ Tbsp vegetable oil
2 tsp matcha + 4 tsp hot water
8 cupcake holders

1. Combine the hotcake mix with the milk, sugar, raisins, and oil, and mix until smooth.

2. Mix the matcha and water and stir briskly until the paste becomes smooth. Add to the hotcake mixture and blend well.

3. Pour the mixture into the cupcake holders, and place in a steamer to cook at high heat for 15 minutes.

Matcha Tiramisu

INGREDIENTS ──────────────── serves 4

7 oz (200 g) mascarpone cheese

3 Tbsp sugar

1 cup fresh cream, whipped

2 Tbsp matcha + 4 Tbsp hot water

1 Tbsp Grand Marnier, Curaçao, or any other liqueur

5–6 slices sponge cake (10 oz/280 g)

½ tsp matcha and a sprig of fresh tea leaves or mint

1. Take the mascarpone cheese out of the refrigerator 20 minutes or so before use. When soft, place in a bowl and whisk until creamy. Add the sugar and whisk again.

2. Put the cream in another bowl, place bowl in a larger bowl of iced water, and whisk the cream until it has the same texture as the mascarpone. Lightly fold into the cheese.

3. Mix the matcha and hot water and stir briskly until the paste becomes smooth. Add some liqueur.

4. Cut the sponge cake into bite-size cubes and sprinkle matcha paste on top.

5. Place two or three pieces in a serving dish and cover with whipped cream and cheese. Add another layer of sponge cake and cream. Repeat the process to make 4 servings.

6. Refrigerate. When cold, serve with a garnish of matcha powder and fresh tea leaves or mint.

Matcha Fruit Bavarois

INGREDIENTS ———————————————— serves 4

1 oz (30 g) powdered gelatin
4 Tbsp water
3 egg yolks
$\frac{1}{2}$ cup sugar
1 tsp cornstarch
pinch of salt
$1\frac{1}{4}$ cups milk
1 Tbsp matcha
1 Tbsp brandy
1 cup fresh cream
strawberries, canned peaches, grapes, or
    any fresh fruit
syrup to taste

1. In a bowl, mix the gelatin and water, place the bowl in a pan of hot water, and mix until the gelatin dissolves.

2. In a separate bowl, combine the egg yolks, sugar, cornstarch, and salt, and stir until the mixture turns whitish.

3. Heat the milk in a small pan until it is lukewarm.

4. Mix the matcha and 2 tablespoons of warm milk and stir briskly until the paste becomes smooth. Set aside.

5. Add the rest of the milk to the egg yolks and cook over low heat, taking care not to let the milk boil as the yolks will harden. Remove from the heat and cool slightly.

6. Add the gelatin, matcha paste, and brandy to the milk, and mix. Place in a large bowl of iced water to let it cool.

7. Lightly whip the cream and fold into the mixture. Pour into individual glasses and refrigerate until set.

8. Serve garnished with your favorite fruit and syrup.

Note
The bavarois will look more attractive if you slightly tilt the glasses when you put them in the refrigerator.

Yogurt Jello with Matcha Syrup

INGREDIENTS ──────────────── serves 4

YOGURT JELLO

   1¼ cups plain yogurt
   1 oz (30 g) powdered gelatin
   4 Tbsp water
   1¼ cups milk
   1 cup sugar
   1 Tbsp lemon juice
   lemon essence
   fresh fruit, any kind

MATCHA SYRUP

   ½ cup sugar
   1 cup water
   pinch of salt
   2 tsp matcha + 4 tsp hot water

1. Take the yogurt out of the refrigerator 20 minutes or so before use.

2. In a bowl, mix the gelatin and water, place the bowl in a pan of hot water, and mix until the gelatin dissolves.

3. Stir the yogurt until smooth. Add the milk, sugar, lemon juice, lemon essence, and gelatin, and mix.

4. Pour into a rectangular pan to let the mixture cool. Refrigerate until it sets (about 4 hours).

5. Make the syrup by combining the sugar and water in a small pan and heating it until the sugar dissolves. Add salt and let it cool.

6. Mix the matcha and water and stir briskly until the paste becomes smooth. Add to the syrup and place in the refrigerator to chill.

7. Cut the jello into ½-inch (1-cm) cubes. Serve in a glass with matcha syrup and your favorite fruit.

Note
For the best flavor, add the syrup just before eating.

PART 4

OTHER FACTS ABOUT TEA

Common Questions about Green Tea

Here are some answers to the most frequently asked questions about green tea.

Q | Is there a way of telling which tea is good?

There is no better way than to sample teas yourself. Some tea shops, such as ITO EN in Manhattan, provide in-house tea experts you can consult. Even if tasting the tea is not possible, you can ask to see and smell the leaves. High-quality teas are dark green and should be tightly rolled, thin, and firm, with a good aroma. To test the quality, put some leaves in your mouth and bite to judge the sweetness, astringency, and flavor.

Q | Are pesticides used in cultivating tea in Japan? Is there a problem with residual chemicals?

Japan's regulations regarding harmful pesticides are probably the severest in the world. Both the Food Sanitation Law of the Ministry of Health, Labor, and Welfare and the safety standards in the Agricultural Chemicals Control Law of the same ministry prohibit the use of harmful pesticides. Farmers cultivate safe and tasty tea by avoiding all unnecessary spraying of chemicals. In addition, organic cultivation is spreading and the use of pesticides is decreasing.

Q | Is there much caffeine in tea?

Yes, there is. Most people know from their own experience that drinking tea keeps them awake. Caffeine stimulates the central nervous system (including the brain cells) and the muscular system, thereby improving blood circulation, which in turn helps the body recover from fatigue. The kind of tea most effective for this is gyokuro, which has a high caffeine content and is therefore an ideal drink when working or studying. Gyokuro is said to be three times as effective as black tea in this respect.

Q | Is it true that medication should not be taken with tea?

Yes, it is best avoided. The caffeine in tea can either weaken or strengthen the effects of medication. For example, painkillers, tranquilizers, and sleeping pills are less effective when taken with tea, and the effect of headache pills and cold remedies may be increased to an undesirable extent. Moreover, tannin combines easily with iron, so the effectiveness of hematinics needed by people suffering from anemia, as well as of medication for digestive ailments, will decrease if taken together with tea.

Q | Is tea really effective against constipation?

Yes. Tea helps to relax the intestines, making it effective for constipation caused by changes of environment, such as when traveling, rather than chronic constipation due to lack of vegetables, fibers, and so on. For people who suffer from constipation or who experience stress-related stomach problems, such as before taking examinations, a cup of green tea will have a calming physical and mental effect.

Q | Why is hojicha served in hospitals in Japan?

Hojicha contains less caffeine and tannin than other types of tea, which means it does not counteract the effectiveness of medicines. It also contains a relatively large amount of vitamin P, which strengthens the walls of blood vessels and also helps in post-operative healing, particularly with patients who run the risk of strokes due to high blood pressure. Another benefit of hojicha is that it prevents halitosis and refreshes the mouth.

Q | What does the Japanese proverb "Don't drink overnight tea" mean?

"Overnight tea" refers to tea made from leaves left in the pot from the previous day. There are two reasons for not reusing the leaves. First, the protein in tea, if left for long periods at a high temperature, fosters the growth of mold. Second, the tea might upset your stomach because of the tannin remaining in it. It is best to start the day with tea that is freshly made.

Q | Is tea good for hangovers?

Yes. Tea's detoxification potential counteracts the effects of alcohol, which is why drinking tea has been regarded as a traditional antidote for hangovers. The moderate stimulation provided by the caffeine settles the mind and helps the body recover from fatigue, and vitamin C helps the function of caffeine. Two or three cups of the first serving of gyokuro or sencha will be best because they contain a lot of both caffeine and vitamin C.

Q | Which contains more vitamin C—citrus fruit, spinach, or tea?

People usually believe that, among natural produce, oranges, lemons, and spinach have the highest concentration of vitamin C, but that honor actually belongs to sencha, $3\frac{1}{2}$ oz (100 g) of which contains a little more than five times the amount of vitamin C in a lemon and a little under three times the amount in spinach. Moreover, the vitamin C in green tea is retained as the steaming process kills the oxidizing enzyme that would otherwise destroy the vitamin C.

Q | Why is the first tea of the season regarded as something special?

The first tea of the season refers to the first tender, immature leaves and needle-shaped shoots that are picked soon after they appear. They are highly valued because they are picked by hand. This first tea is bright in color and has a refreshing aroma.

Q | Why does the tea served in sushi restaurants seem so flavorful?

The tea served at sushi restaurants has a distinctive flavor and aroma, and is drunk between servings of different types of fish and shellfish to refresh the palate. The restaurants use konacha (tea powder), which is what is sifted out in the processing of sencha or gyokuro. It is reasonably priced in Japan and is gradually becoming popular in homes as well.

Q | Can strong tea upset your stomach?

Yes, that is possible. Tea of normal strength functions in various ways, such as stimulating the stomach and encouraging the secretion of the gastric juices necessary for digestion. It will not damage the stomach. However, strong tea can overstimulate the stomach because of the tannin and caffeine. You should avoid drinking tea that is so strong and thick that the bottom of the teacup is obscured. People with weak stomachs are advised not to drink tea when they are hungry.

Q | Is there any difference between Japanese green tea and green tea from China and other countries?

All teas come from one species of tea plant. However, there are many subspecies of the plant. The flavors and colors of Japanese green tea, Chinese oolong tea, or black tea are the result of different processing methods that control the degree of fermentation.

After the tea leaves are plucked, the tannin gradually starts to oxidize, which causes the leaves to ferment. To halt that process, green tea in Japan is steamed or roasted to produce unfermented tea. Semifermented tea, such as oolong tea, is roasted before complete fermentation has occurred. Black tea has undergone complete fermentation.

Q | What is the best way to store tea?

Tea readily absorbs water and is easily affected by heat and temperature, so it should be stored in a cool, dry place. The refrigerator is ideal, but be sure that the tea container has a tight lid to prevent the tea absorbing smells from other items.

If the tea is stored in a refrigerator or freezer for a long time, the smell of the tea may permeate the refrigerator. Thus, it is better to buy tea in small quantities, purchasing only the amount that you will drink in the near future. Before storing, the tea should be well wrapped in plastic.

Q | What is "benifuki" tea and can it really reduce allergic symptoms?

"Benifuki" is a type of tea made available in 1993 by the National Agricultural Research Organization of the National Institute of Vegetable and Tea Science in Japan. A substance called "methylated catechin," which reduces allergic symptoms, was discovered in the tea catechins responsible for the astringent component in tea. Benifuki tea contains more of this substance than other teas and demand for it is expected to increase.

Q Is there a good way of removing tea stains?

Tea vessels become stained over time, but a kitchen cleanser or bleach can remove the stains. However, the patina of tea stains that develops on some porcelain utensils over years of use is regarded as desirable. In China, in particular, this patina is cherished because it shows that the vessels have been used with care for a long time.

Health Benefits of Green Tea

Science has been continuously revealing the benefits of tea. The green tea drunk daily in Japan is now touted as one of the healthiest drinks in the world. Listed here are some of the benefits.

⬥ Aids the body's pH balance and overall functioning

A healthy body is slightly alkaline, but an unbalanced diet of too many calories makes it more acidic. Tea, an alkaline product rich in minerals, counteracts acidity. Moreover, since green tea has no calories, weight gain is not a worry. The minerals in tea—potassium, sodium, calcium, manganese, copper, zinc, nickel, and molybdenum—help the body to function well.

⬥ Aids digestion

When first introduced to Japan, green tea was drunk both to keep awake and as an aid to digestion since the tannin stimulates the stomach and increases intestinal activity. Green tea can benefit those with a tendency to be constipated.

⬥ Refreshes body and mind

One component of green tea is caffeine, which helps to dispel drowsiness and lassitude. A cup of tea drunk during work will clear the head and refresh both body and mind. Incidentally, the caffeine in green tea is a milder form than that present in coffee because it is combined with catechins.

⬥ Prevents illness

Vitamin C builds up resistance to infections, thereby preventing colds and other common ailments. Tea boosts the immune system and strengthens the constitution, helping the body to combat stress.

✈ Promotes healthy skin tone

Vitamin C is essential for good skin tone with a youthful elasticity. The vitamin C in green tea is resistant to heat, and can withstand temperatures as high as 176° F (80° C). Moreover, green tea is so rich in vitamin C that three cups of sencha contain the same amount of vitamin C as an apple.

✈ Aids weight loss

Dieting has become popular in Japan and other advanced countries where too many rich meals and fast foods are consumed. However, people on diets often drink special "diet teas," which have adverse effects. In fact, ordinary green tea is preferable to diet teas. Green tea has no calories and is drunk without sugar. Moreover, if green tea is drunk after a rich meal, its tannin content helps the fat-degrading enzymes to work better. A cup of tea drunk before a meal can alleviate hunger and provide the vitamins and minerals that tend to be lacking in many diet drinks. So when you're on a diet, drink more green tea than usual!

✈ Provides much-needed zinc for expectant mothers

The chief concern of a mother-to-be is the health of her unborn child. A survey on the connection between a lack of minerals—especially zinc and copper—and low birth weight has been drawing attention recently in Europe and the United States. Zinc is a mineral that is needed during pregnancy and is present in green tea, so expectant mothers are recommended to drink some green tea each day.

✈ Inhibits carcinogens

The catechins contained in tea leaves can suppress carcinogens and inhibit cancer-causing agents in cell growth. What's more, green tea is rich in other components believed to help prevent cancer, including carotene, vitamin C, vitamin E, and dietary fiber.[1]

✈ Lowers cholesterol levels

Tea catechins reduce "bad cholesterol," or low-density lipoprotein-cholesterol (LDL cholesterol), in the blood, thereby preventing hardening of the arteries and the formation of blood clots.[2]

✈ Lowers high blood pressure

Tea catechins inhibit the function of the angiotensin I–converting enzyme (ACE) that produces angiotensin II, which is responsible for high blood pressure. Thus, catechins can prevent high blood pressure. Gaba Tea is considered the most effective; it contains several dozen times more γ-amino butyric acid (GABA)—a substance produced from glutamic acid, which is one of the flavor-enhancing ingredients of tea—than regular teas.[3]

Prevents diabetes

Tea catechins lower blood sugar levels by inhibiting the action of amylase, an enzyme that breaks down starches such as carbohydrates and converts them into glucose. The dark color of black tea is the result of oxidization of the catechins, so black tea theaflavins are also effective in preventing diabetes.[4]

In addition to catechins, water-soluble polysaccharides in tea—consisting of combined saccharides including arabinose, glycose, and ribose—have also been found to lower the blood sugar level.[5]

Slows the aging process

Tea catechins prevent the oxidation of fat in foods, and are thus natural antioxidant agents. Among them, epigallo catechin gallate (EGCG) has about twenty times the antioxidant power of vitamin E.[6]

Tea is an antioxidant substance, and the carotene, vitamin C, and vitamin E give it a synergistic effect. Thus, it slows aging and also inhibits the growth of can-cer-causing agents in cells.

Prevents food poisoning

The epigallo catechins in tea are considered effective in preventing food poison-ing because of their antibacterial and antitoxin capabilities.[7]

The theaflavins in black tea have an antibacterial and antitoxin effect equal to the catechins in green tea, and it has been proved that theaflavins are also effective against vibrio cholera.[8]

Theaflavins ensure the freshness of food. If fish is dipped in cold tea before it is cooked, or if tea is sprinkled over the cooked fish, the theaflavins will be effec-tive in halting an increase in bacteria and thus preventing food poisoning.

Protects against colds

Tea is also effective in weakening the influenza virus. For that reason, gargling with tea offers an effective protection against colds.[9]

Prevents tooth decay

Tea catechins prevent the growth of bacteria that causes tooth decay and also the formation of plaque. In addition, the fluoride in tea helps to strengthen tooth enamel.[10]

Prevents halitosis

Tea catechins are effective against the periodontal bacteria that cause halitosis. Rinsing the mouth with a solution of tea will suppress halitosis.

⧸ Removes tobacco stains

Green tea can help to remove tobacco stains from teeth since both green tea catechins and black tea theaflavins tend to bond with tars.[11]

1. From a study by Professor Itaro Oguni et al., Department of Food and Nutrition, Shizuoka University Junior College.
2. In laboratory rat cases—from a study by Prof. Keiichiro Muramatsu of Nagoya Women's University and Yukihiko Hara, Food Research Labs., Mitsui Norin Co., Ltd.; in human cases—from a study by Setsuko Kanaya, a dietician at Seirei Mikatahara Hospital, in Hamamatsu, Shizuoka Prefecture.
3. From a study by Yukihiko Hara, Food Research Labs., Mitsui Norin Co., Ltd., et al.
4. From studies by Professor Masuji Minowada of Kyoto University, Yukihiko Hara, Food Research Labs., Mitsui Norin Co., Ltd., et al.
5. From a study by Prof. Mineo Shimizu, Toyama Medical and Pharmaceutical University.
6. From a study by Professors Takuo Okuda and Hikoya Hayatsu, et al., Faculty of Pharmaceutical Sciences, Okayama University.
7. Hara, et al.
8. From a study by Professor Tadakatsu Shimamura et al., Medical Department of Showa University.
9. Ibid.
10. Hara, et al.
11. Fumio Okada, a researcher at the National Institute of Vegetable and Tea Science, presently at Food Research Labs., Mitsui Norin Co., Ltd.

Note

"Health Benefits of Green Tea" was condensed from text in *Ocha: Oishii Kusuri* (Green Tea: Delicious Medicine) by Itaro Oguni and Mutsuko Tokunaga.

Classic Green Tea Labels

Japan began exporting green tea in 1859, and with brands such as Shogun and Samurai took full advantage of its cultural heritage to attract attention overseas.

Useful Household Tips with Green Tea

We live in a throw-away society, but many things we dispose of each day can have other uses, such as old tea leaves. These traditional household tips have been handed down from generation to gereneration in Japan and are still useful even today.

As a deodorizer

Used tea leaves make good odor-removers for refrigerators and wardrobes. First dry the leaves thoroughly and then wrap them in a gauze bag.

The leaves can be taken out periodically and dry-roasted in a fry pan to revive their deodorizing function, but be careful not to burn them. If you wrap the leaves in a decorative cloth, you will have an attractive display item.

As a fertilizer

Squeeze all the water out of old tea leaves and bury them in the soil next to the roots of plants and bushes. They are great for indoor plants, too. After some time you will notice the leaves looking brighter.

For a finger bowl

After handling fish, you can clean your hands by rubbing them with used tea leaves to remove fishy smells. In the same way, after eating crab or prawns, rinse your hands in a bowl of tea. Tea leaves will also remove grease from your hands after handling meat.

For diaper rash and bedsores

After the first serving, pour more hot water on the leaves and then pour this into another container to let it cool to the baby's body temperature. Dip a piece of soft gauze in the tea, squeeze it lightly, and wipe the affected areas. This method is also effective against bedsores.

For treating cuts

Chew the used tea leaves a little to soften them, and then apply to minor cuts such as those sustained working in the kitchen. This will stop the bleeding, and the tannin acts as a disinfectant.

For morning sickness

For many pregnant women, nibbling on steeped leaves, especially those with a high content of vitamin C, such as quality sencha, can relieve morning sickness.

As bath salts

Used tea leaves wrapped in gauze and placed in the bath emit a rich aroma that will help soothe your body and mind. Tea leaves are also said to improve the complexion, but please be aware that tea will stain towels.

For athlete's foot and hemorrhoids

Apply softened tea leaves to those parts of your feet affected with athlete's foot, or apply a gauze soaked in strong bancha, changing it several times a day. If the infection is still at an early stage, this is an effective remedy because of the antiseptic quality of tannin. Inflammation between the fingers, caused when the hands are immersed in water for a long time, seems to heal quickly if the fingers are soaked in bancha for about ten minutes and then dried. In mild cases of hemorrhoids, washing with lukewarm bancha is said to provide relief from itchiness.

For producing dyes

Just as you can produce dyes with herbs, you can make a pale green dye by adding powdered green tea to water and boiling it to reduce the liquid.

For stuffing pillows

Pillows stuffed with used tea leaves that have been thoroughly dried in the sun are said to prevent hot flushes and improve blood circulation.

As first aid after a tooth extraction

Tannin has an antiseptic effect, so rinsing your mouth with strong bancha will help to stop the bleeding after a tooth has been extracted.

Tea and Proverbs

Green tea features in many Japanese proverbs and sayings that have great charm. Here are a few examples with their literal translations, followed by an explanation of the meaning.

Asacha wa nan o nogareru.

Drinking tea in the morning before you go out avoids trouble.

This proverb suggests that because drinking tea is refreshing and calming, you can avoid getting involved in disputes or trouble by drinking tea in the morning, before you go out or start work.

Oni mo juhachi, bancha mo debana.

A devil is eighteen, bancha is really fresh.

"*Debana*" means freshly served tea. Lower-grade bancha, which is produced from leftover leaves and stalks, still tastes good if served fresh. The proverb means that even a woman with plain looks becomes beautiful in her own way when she reaches marriageable age.

Oyaji wa shibucha, ofukuro wa amacha nari.

Father is like bitter tea, Mother like sweet tea.

In the old days it was always father who scolded the kids and mother who gave them pocket money. Today, perhaps it is the other way around.

Chabashira ga tatsu to engi ga yoi.

It's a good sign if a tea stem floats upright in your cup.

A tea stem floating upright in your morning tea is believed to be an omen of good luck for the day. A stem floating in the center of your cup indicates great good fortune. This is a favorite proverb of speculators and of geisha. It is also believed that your luck will increase if you do not tell anyone about this. An upright stem later in the day denotes luck for someone close to you. So carefully check your teacup!

Ocha ni yotta furi.

Pretending to be drunk with tea.

This means fooling others by pretending not to know anything, like pretending to be drunk without having had any alcohol.

Ocha o nigosu.
To make the tea turbid.

This means to speak ambiguously or to mislead.

Chacha o ireru.
To put in the tea.

This expression means to interrupt someone or throw cold water on a scheme.

Ocha to jo wa koigoi to.
Tea and the heart are better strong and deep.

This reflects the belief that it is impolite to serve weak tea to guests.

Orokanaru otto o moteba cha mo hiyuru.
If your husband is a fool, even the tea gets cold.

This means that you will lose a good chance if you are too slow.

Nichijo sahanji.

"Nichijo" means "daily life," and "sahanji" means "to drink tea and eat dinner." In other words, tea should be a vital part of our everyday lives.

CREDITS

Mizuho Kuwata, pp. 1–10, 13–15, 18–19, 20 (top), 22, 24–37, 48, 50, 56–57, 64–65, 114

Kenji Shinohara, pp. 17, 38, 39 (bottom), 41–42, 45–47, 66–67, 70–77, 82–113

Itsuo Mitsui, pp. 11, 16, 20 (bottom), 39 (top), 40, 51, 78–81

Agency for Cultural Affairs, Japan and Kyoto National Museum, pp. 58–59, *Autumn Moon on Lake Dongting (Eight Views of the Xiao Xian),* by Yu Jian

Leiden National Museum of Ethnology, pp. 53–55, the processing of green tea, from the Siebold Collections

Tekisui Museum of Art, p. 58, *Lu Yu,* by Chikuden Tanomura

Tokyo National Museum, p. 60, Chinese landscape, by Ike no Taiga; p. 62, *Waitress, Kasamori Osen* by Harunobu Suzuki; p. 128, *Waitress Okita of Naniwaya* by Utamaro Kitagawa

Yokohama Archives of History, pp. 122–23, tea labels

Chocolates, pp. 8–9, 34, 50: Pierre Marcolini, Ginza

Drinks, p. 36: Asahi Breweries, Ltd.; Ito En, Ltd.; Kirin Brewery Co., Ltd.; Sapporo Breweries Limited; Suntory Limited

The author and publisher wish to acknowledge the following cafes, companies, shops, and associations:

ITO EN, New York • mentioned on page 32
822 Madison Avenue (between 68th and 69th Streets), New York, New York 10021
Tel: 212–988–7111; restaurant **KAI**, Tel: 212–988–7277
The shop and restaurant are closed Sundays. Internet access: www.itoen.com

CHA GINZA • photos on back jacket (top), pp. 2–5, 8–9, 13–15,22–31, 32 (top, bottom)
5–5–6 Ginza, Chuo-ku, Tokyo 104–0061
Tel: 03–3571–1211 • Closed Mondays

TORAYA CAFÉ • photos on front jacket, pp. 6–7, 10, 32 (center), 33, 35, 37, 114
6–12–2 Roppongi-keyakizakadori, Roppongi-Hills Roppongi, Minato-ku, Tokyo 106–0032
Tel: 03–5786–9811 • Internet access: www.toraya-cafe.co.jp

TORAYA Paris • mentioned on page 32
10, Rue St-Florentin, 75001 Paris
Tel: 01 42 60 13 00 • Open everyday except Sundays or national holidays

World Green Tea Association (Japan)
Tel: 054–221–3641, Fax: 054–221–2299
Internet access: www.o-cha.net
E-mail: ryokucha@hq.pref.shizuoka.jp

Japan Tea Central Association
Contact sugimoto@nihoncha-inst.com for general questions or guidelines for becoming a Japanese Green Tea Advisor or Japanese Green Tea Instructor

(英文版)日本茶。—新しい魅力と愉しみ方
New Tastes in Green Tea

2004年3月5日　第1刷発行

著　者　　徳永睦子
撮　影　　桑田瑞穂、篠原健二
訳　者　　ステュウット・アットキン、とよざきようこ
発行者　　畑野文夫
発行所　　講談社インターナショナル株式会社
　　　　　〒112-8652　東京都文京区音羽 1-17-14
　　　　　電話　03-3944-6493（編集部）
　　　　　　　　03-3944-6492（営業部・業務部）
　　　　　ホームページ　www.kodansha-intl.co.jp

印刷・製本所　　大日本印刷株式会社